# *KAILASH:*
# Impressions and Expressions

# *KAILASH*:
# Impressions and Expressions

Dr. Manoj M. Haridas

GYAN

GYAN PUBLISHING HOUSE

NEW DELHI-110002

***KAILASH:***
**Impressions and Expressions**
*(Tourism. Religion. Geology. History, Botany. Mountaineering, Tibetology)*

ISBN : 81-212-0569-7



Published in 1997 in India by
Gyan Publishing House
5, Ansari Road
New Delhi 110 002



Laser Typeset at Grow Computers, Delhi.
Printed at Mehra Offset Press, New Delhi.

# Contents

*List of Illustrations* 7

*List of Tables* 11

*List of Maps* 13

*Preface* 15

*Acknowledgements* 17

**1. Kailash and Manasarovar for the Beginner** 19

Why Trek to Kailash-Manasarovar?, Kailash-Manasarovar: A Brief Background, How is the Kailash-Manasarovar Trek Different from Others?, The Trekking Route: A Short Description, Don't go with Statistics. Go with an Attitude, Tangible Gains from a Trek to Kailash-Manasarovar.

**2. Adventure in the Kailash-Manasarovar Region : Theory and Practice** 31

Routes to Kailash-Manasarovar from India, Routes to Kailash-Manasarovar from the far North, The Absence of Informative Trekking Maps on the Region, Kailash-Manasarovar along the Lipulekh-Gurla Mandhata Corridor, Planning the Trek upto a 10,000 feet altitude (Delhi to Gunji), Administrative Protocols, New Delhi to Almora, Almora to Dharchula, Dharchula to Tawaghat, Tawaghat to Pangu, Pangu to Sirkha via Narayan Ashram, Sirkha to Gala, Gala to Malpa, Malpa to Budhi, Flora at the Budhi Camp, Budhi to Gunji, On Gunji.

**3. Trekking in the High Altitudes (Gunji and Beyond)** 65

Gunji to Kalapani, Kalapani to Navidang, Navidang to Lipulekh Pass, On Lipulekh Pass, Waiting at Lipulekh, Towards Taklakot.

**4. On the Tibetan Plateau** 79

Getting Used to Different Time Zones, What to See and What to Buy in Taklakot, A Bit of Indian Heritage in Taklakot, Telephoning India from Taklakot, Separation of Groups in Taklakot, Planning for the Next Eight Days.

**5. The Kailash Parikrama** 89

Tarchen to Direbu, Some Tips on How to Handle Yaks, Approaching Direbu, Direbu to Zongzerbu, Zongzerbu to Tarchen.

**6. The Manasarovar Parikrama** 105

Tarchen to Horche, Horche to Chugu, Chugu to Zaidi, The Enigma of the Rakshas Tal, On Khojarnath, A Summary of the Kailash-Manasarovar Yatra.

*Bibliography* 115

*Index* 121

# List of Illustrations


Fig. 1. An altitude-distance-trekking route sketch of the Kailash-Manasarovar Yatra, from start to finish.

Fig. 2. A Destination-Distance-Altitude-Inclination sketch of the trekking route to Kailash-Manasarovar.

Fig. 3. The 6 km horizontal stretch along a one km vertical ascent, from Tawaghat to Pangu, known locally as *Thanedar ki Chadhai,* is one of the stiffest ascents throughout the journey, and can pose a formidable challenge even to an experienced trekker.

Fig. 4. In the left of the photograph is the Dhauliganga river gorge. Observe the greenery caused by the first rains and note the landslide on the left river bank, in front of the trekkers.

Fig. 5. The main prayer hall at the Narayan Ashram. The Ashram is located between Pangu and Sirkha.

Fig. 6. A photograph showing the turbulent Kaliganga river and its confluence with a rivulet from Nepal.

Fig. 7. A panoramic view of Najung Jharana from Najunggarh.

Fig. 8. The Chrysalis Imperialis rose photographed near Budhi.

Fig. 9. The Himalayan Knotweed seen in the vicinity of the KMVN Camp at Budhi.

Fig. 10. The Himalayan Hogweed seen on the mountain slopes near Budhi.

Fig. 11. The Himalayan Betony seen on wet mountain slopes near the KMVN camp at Budhi.

Fig. 12. The Jack-in the-Pulpit photographed in the neighbourhood of KMVN Camp at Budhi.

Fig. 13. A section of the trek over a plasticized clayey patch, vertically over the Kaliganga embankment.

Fig. 14. A view of the turbulent Kaliganga river between Budhi and Gunji.

Fig. 15. Another view of the turbulent Kaliganga between Budhi and Gunji.

Fig. 16. A view of the mating mountain ranges in the neighbourhood of the KMVN camp at Gunji (10,625ft.)

Fig. 17. A Destination-Distance-Altitude-Inclination map of the Indian section of the Kailash-Manasarovar Yatra.

Fig. 18. A Nepali house photographed over the Kaliganga river.

Fig. 19. A view of the Vyas mountains from the KMVN Camp at Kalapani.

Fig. 20. A view of the Shiva-Parvati-Vaishnodevi temple at Kalapani. The Kaliganga originates in the rocks behind the temple.

Fig. 21. An unusual tree formation along the Kalapani-Navidang trekking route.

Fig. 22. A view of the barren mountains between Kalapani and Navidang.

Fig. 23. A set of weather conditions which mask the *Om* on the Om-Parvat.

Fig. 24. The Om-Parvat in its fullest grandeur on a clear day. Observe the *Om* in Devanagari inscribed into the mountains and embossed in snow.

Fig. 25. Trekkers descending from India into Tibet over the Lipulekh Pass.

Fig. 26. The Tibetan side of the Lipulekh Pass. It is a steep uphill into India.

Fig. 27. A Chinese Bank in Taklakot which remains open upto 8.30 p.m. even on Sundays.

Fig. 28. A Destination-Distance-Altitude-Inclination map of the Tibetan section of the Kailash-Manasarovar Yatra.

Fig. 29. The western face of Mount Kailash from near the Choku Gompa, midway between Tarchen and Direbu.

Fig. 30. The northern face of Kailash photographed from the camp at Direbu.

Fig. 31. A fuller view of the North face of Mount Kailash from Direbu.

Fig. 32. A view of the "flaming red" Mount Kailash at sunrise. The sun's rays need to strike the plano-convex region of Kailash's north face at a precise grazing incidence. The result is a brilliant golden hue and the mountain emanates a beacon-like radiance which can be seen from several hundred miles. Verily enough, this is Kailash in all its grandeur. Men with better vocabularies and richer thought have written poems in praise of the sight.

Fig. 33. Dolma Pass—The High Point in the Kailash-Manasarovar Yatra (19,800 ft.).

Fig. 34. A view of the Gauri Kund along the descent from the Dolma Pass.

Fig. 35. A view of the Southern face of Mount Kailash, with two faces inscribed on the right on the snowy dome. Observe with deliberation, the well formed eyes and the eyebrows, the delicately shaped nose, the lips as well as a chin on each face. I would say the face on the left belongs to Lord Shiva and the one on the right to Goddess Parvati. But don't ask me for explanations as to how these inscriptions got there. I don't know! Maybe, there is a supernatural.

Fig. 36. The Gurla Mandhata and its reflection in the Lake Manasarovar.

Fig. 37. Lake Manasarovar in the foreground and Mount Kailash in the backdrop. The mountain is at least 80 km away from the point of photography.

Fig. 38. Ducks and Barred Geese seen paddling in the cool waters of the Manasarovar.

Fig. 39. Manasarovar in another of its many moods, colours and costumes.

Fig. 40. The religious dip into the Manasarovar is said to wash off the sins of seven generations. The eighth generation very nearly dies of cold in the noble attempt.

Fig. 41. A view of the Rakshas Tal from near the Kosu monastery.

Fig. 42. The inner sanctum of the Ram-Laxman-Sita temple at Khojarnath.

# List of Tables

1. A step-by-step Destination-Distance-Altitude account of the Kailash-Manasarovar Yatra. This table may be used as a ready reckoner. 26

2. Different routes to Kailash and Manasarovar from India. Several fair-weather, non-permanent, the most difficult routes to Tarchen arriving from the North also exist which were used by the Russian and Mongol explorers and expeditions. 32

# List of Maps


1. A primitive trekking map of Mount Kailash and its immediate neighbourhood. BETWEEN 92 AND 93
2. A primitive trekking map of Lake Manasarovar and its immediate neighbourhood. BETWEEN 106 AND 107

# Preface

When saddled with the responsibility of writing a preface for this book, I feel a little like Tom Sawyer. The incident which at once comes to mind is the series of events which led Tom to claim a copy of the Holy Bible in exchange for ten red coupons. I have a very hearty laugh every time I read Mark Twain and despite instructions to be brief, I will try to build up the episode with the hope that it will make the drawing of parallels simpler.

Tom Sawyer was a street-smart school kid, much like Top Cat on the Cartoon Network. Usually, he was at the bottom of his class in academics but an absolute super achiever when it came to thinking on his feet. The village *padre* who also taught the Moral Sciences at Tom's school, introduced a coupon system to foster religious learning. One yellow coupon signified that the bearer had fully understood and memorised one psalm. Ten yellow coupons could be exchanged for one blue coupon and ten blue ones equalled a red one. A wad of ten red backs entitled the bearer to a Holy Bible and a felicitation at a formal ceremony. In this competition, a young German lad was the top seed and, given his past record, Tom was knocked out of the contest even before it began. But Tom had an inventiveness which everybody else lacked. When his grandmother asked him to whitewash the house and the fence, Tom positioned the burdensome task so that it appeared to be a privilege and a form of reward for extraordinary merit. Very soon, he had his classmates begging him to allow them to paint. Naturally, he had put a price on whitewashing privileges. The service charge was one yellow coupon. Before the day was out, Tom had turned capitalist and the fence was painted several times over. The German lad gladly paid to work. At the next Sunday school, Tom put forth his claim for the Bible. The chaplain froze on the spot for, in Twain's own words: "he hadn't been expecting an application from this source for the next hundred years".

And this is exactly the point that I wish to make. To my professors, employers, clients, colleagues and friends, I was the last person expected to write populist adventure literature on the Himalayas. Three months before I went to Manasarovar, I would have struggled to locate Lipulekh

Pass on a World Map. I went to Tibet only because at that time, I had nothing else to do. And when the trekking began, I started taking notes and recording observations as a means to spend time between an evening tea and sunset.

Documentation can be very habit forming and soon, I found my writing activity to extend to well past dinner times. Every day and throughout the 32-day trek, there appeared to be more and more to write about, to photograph, to experience, to breathe and to "communionise" (if I may be permitted to coin a word here). When I got back to Mumbai, I discovered that between a few close friends, I had access to over 3000 photographs and over 2000 pages of hand-written first hand reports on the Kailash-Manasarovar Yatra: the most recent being my own and the one of greatest vintage from a certain Mr. Dikshit of Mumbai who traversed the mountains in the early 1940s.

Kailash and Manasarovar were getting to be more appealing and magnetic after my return from Tibet. Within a week of getting back, I found myself wanting to know everything that has ever been written on the subject; be it geology, history, geography, art, botany, movement of tectonic plates, formation of fold mountains or something which I had religiously avoided all along: religion.

Historical tracings went back to the 17th century for literature written in English and to the 13th century for Russian reports which I could neither study nor acquire. At first glance, religious texts appear essentially unchanged over the last few centuries and I must admit I have not researched the religious stock of knowledge into a depth of significance. However, after a few months of reading everything else that I could find, discussing periodically with other trekkers, recording and distilling written notes, this book evolved into the form that you see it in today. To be honest, I experienced a great sense of fulfilment when I read a draft copy some time back. The book was exactly the way I wanted it to be.

It will be very unfair for me to take the full credit for writing this book. A Kailash-Manasarovar adventure book for the amateur trekker was just begging to be written. I only had a compilation of data, facts and information and possibly served as a writing instrument in bringing the demand and the supply together. The complete and simple truth is that book wrote itself and this is the only selling proposition I would like to use in introducing this book to the reader.

25th July 1997 MANOJ M. HARIDAS

# ILLUSTRATIONS

*Fig. 3.*

*Fig. 5.*

Fig. 6.

*Fig. 7.*

*Fig. 8.*

# Acknowledgements

The acknowledgements section has been the easiest to write in the entire book simply because contributions have been extremely specific and have arrived when they were needed the most.

Some of the best photographs in this adventure documentation are from the personal archives of Mr. Vishwas Gore, Mr. Sagar Abhyankar, Mr. Abhay Kane and Ms. Ruchita Dalal, all from Mumbai. Every photograph has been cited and the author wishes to record his thanks to his four colleagues who have been extremely encouraging and unstinting in their enthusiasm and support right from when this manuscript was conceived. After all, enthusiasm is what this book is all about! And enthusiasm is what I have seen all around me; moreso in the early stages of this book's birth. Professor Rajeev M. Haridas painstakingly compiled the Kailash-Manasarovar trekking maps for me and Mr. Abhijit Ranadive, a commercial artist from Mumbai promptly and beautifully sketched them in the while that the publishers were waiting for me to send in the complete document. I hope the quality of my work matches that of the contributions from these men and women.

The seminal work on Kailash-Manasarovar was written way back in 1907 by Professor Sven Hedin. Another brilliant piece of scientific documentation was by Swami Pranavananda in 1936. However today, these books are woefully obsolete and out-of-date. Another factor which has prompted the compilation of this book is that the scientific and religious romance of the region have not been packaged attractively enough to be appealing to the adventurous at heart. The credit for providing tomes and tomes of first rate material to mull through before compilation of this manuscript began, goes to Mr. Hiren Sampat of Mumbai. Mr. Sampat has arguably the most up-to-date and comprehensive library on the subject that I have seen, heard or read about. Most of the material listed in the Bibliography is available with him and it amazes me no end to know that he does something else for a living. When I hear of people who take even their relaxation very seriously, I am at once reminded of Sampat!

I would also like to record my gratitude to Mr. R.D. Vashikar of the Kailash-Manasarovar Yatri Mandal, Mumbai for his encouragement guidance and feedback. At his age, he works like a man on a mission and I have always felt richer on meeting him.

Thanks are also due to Mr. Ajit Gupte, Under Secretary (China), Ministry of External Affairs, New Delhi for his help, warmth and understanding and patience in hearing me through when I was an impatient Kailash-Manasarovar Yatri in 1996.

Before it escapes my attention, I must record my appreciation and gratitude for the jawans and the officers of the Indo-Tibetan Border Police. There is a lot to learn from men who are honest, disciplined and loyal and I feel a lot better having written this sentence than being in a predicament of yet having to do so.

I owe a great deal to my colleagues of Batch 5 of the 1996 Kailash-Manasarovar Yatra. I was privileged to have extremely good company in Mr. Sukumar Das, a Physics school master from Raiganj in West Bengal, Mr. Subrahmanyam, a banker from Hyderabad and Mr. Amit Kumar, a pious businessman from New Delhi. Mr. Satish Kumar, our Liaison Officer was the sort of group leader that every group should necessarily have. Ours was a group of 28 and our company gelled almost instantly. We were beginning to have fun even before we left Delhi. In trekking expeditions which extend to about 35 days or so, the kind of company you have decides many things, including the very success of the sojourn. I must say, we were singularly lucky in this respect.

In my search for scientific literature, I have received great help from the on-line and CD-ROM data bases at the Library Information Services of the Bhabha Atomic Research Centre and the Indian Institute of Technology, Bombay. I thank Mr. Mainkar, Mr. Jadhav and Mrs. Accanoor for their assistance.

Lastly, I am indebted to the average Indian tax-payer who has served to subsidise my religious/adventurous sojourn to Kailash-Manasarovar. Some day, I would like to go to Kailash once again!

I dedicate this work to my parents for reasons I care very deeply about.

# 1

# Kailash and Manasarovar for the Beginner

Let's face it. For an average burdened, constrained, city-dweller, finding time for himself, usually means pursuing whatever hobbies he may have or going to the cinema or taking the children out for a picnic. But is this really what one might call 'finding time for himself'? There is very little introspection and even less of a self-talk or communion involved in any of these exercises. I think it sometimes pays to cut loose from the shackles of the system and temporarily focus your energies elsewhere. In my experience, this results in a renewed appreciation of one's own work. After all, it is part of one's loyalty to his profession to periodically evaluate the quality of his contribution.

I would recommend a trek to Kailash-Manasarovar in Tibet. The 40-day journey is long, demanding and risky. But it is the ultimate in adventure, excitement and trekking achievement. To be able to do it, you need to be free from diabetes and high blood pressure. People from eighteen to eighty who complete the trek find the call of the mountains irrepressible. They keep coming back for more even if it means tearing themselves from their lucrative professions. Judges, doctors, scientists, engineers, journalists, statesmen, writers, industrialists, you name the category, you'll find them all in each group that treks to Manasarovar.

**Why Trek to Kailash-Manasarovar?**

Why do people go to Manasarovar? Historians and geologists

go for research. Botanists and ornithologists go for documentation. The youth go for adventure. The religious go on pilgrimage. The objects may differ but the common thread is that each person goes to 'find time for himself' where he can listen to himself, motivate himself and transform himself into the sort of person he would like himself to be. Manasarovar (which means 'reservoir of the mind') is not a destination. It is a journey and one like no other.

**Kailash-Manasarovar: A Brief Background**

A great many books have been written on the Kailash-Manasarovar region in Tibet's Ali Province right from Professor Sven Hedin's seminal accounts of geophysical research in 1907 and Swami Pranavananda's stimulating treatise on religion and travel, to the extremely bad which I shall not name. However, if there is one common ideology running through all the documented literature on this subject, it is that a religious pursuit often needs the guise of an adventurous spirit, in order to be fulfilling, stimulating and satisfying. In my opinion, all the available information on Kailash-Manasarovar, broadly falls into three categories: the Pranavananda class which is intellectually stimulating and exhaustive, but a little out-of-date, the religious and the sacrosanct class, such as the *Shivank* which is extremely poetic but beyond my comprehension, and lastly, the adventure-book segment, which treats the Yatra more as a romance in adventure with some amount of religious accompaniment.

This book is targeted at addressing the third category of trekkers for whom there is no carry-along reference manual available on adventure bookshelves today.

**How is the Kailash-Manasarovar Trek Different from Others?**

A Kailash Yatra is not the usual sort of trek organised by college adventure clubs or wildlife sororities. It is different in design, content and objectives. The risks and challenges are greater, possibly unequalled, and as a result the sense of achievement and fulfilment are larger. The first difference is felt at Delhi where the "yatris" (I don't agree to the choice of this word, but use it nevertheless, in the absence of a better one) fill in a legal document stating 'the risk is mine, no compensation will be claimed', at the Ministry of External Affairs. I can't think of many other treks where such a certification is necessary.

Routewise, the trek follows the Delhi-Almora-Dharchula-Gunji-Lipulekh-Taklakot-Manasarovar-Kailash and back trail, with a maximum altitude attained at 19,800 feet (Dolma Pass during the Kailash parikrama), the maximum distance travelled of 42 km in a single day, between Horche and Chugu during the Manasarovar parikrama, the Navidang-Lipulekh stretch awaited with most trepidation, the Gala-Malpa section which induces the greatest fear of death (and a consequent belief in God) and the Tawaghat-Pangu stretch, on the first day of trekking, which tests a yatris mettle and mental make-up. A graphical overview of the route from New Delhi to Kailash-Manasarovar and back, for readers keen on 'all trekking information at a glance' is presented in Fig. 1.

Fig. 1 is a graphical sketch of the altitudes attained and distances travelled in the Kailash-Manasarovar Yatra, starting from New Delhi and reaching Manasarovar and Kailash via Almora, Dharchula, Gunji and Lipulekh. The return journey follows the same route back. The total journey is 2014 km of which the first 657 km from New Delhi to Tawaghat (along the Almora-Dharchula route), and the final 657 km from Tawaghat to New Delhi are by bus (i. e. a total of 1314 km of bus journey in India, plus another 385 km in Tibet, which makes a total of 1701 km out of 2014 km by bus, or approximately 85 per cent of the entire trek. It is the remaining 15 per cent of the route which provides the excitement, the thrill, the adventure and the risk. Every single kilometre to be walked, about 315 of them in all, has a story to tell). The highest altitude attained in the trek is at the Dolma Pass, 19, 800 feet, during the Kailash parikrama. The dome-like peak of Kailash towers over the Dolma Pass. In this sketch, the height of the Kailash is compared with that of the Gurla Mandhata (which is the tallest mountain in the Kailash range) and also with Mount Everest. Each prominent

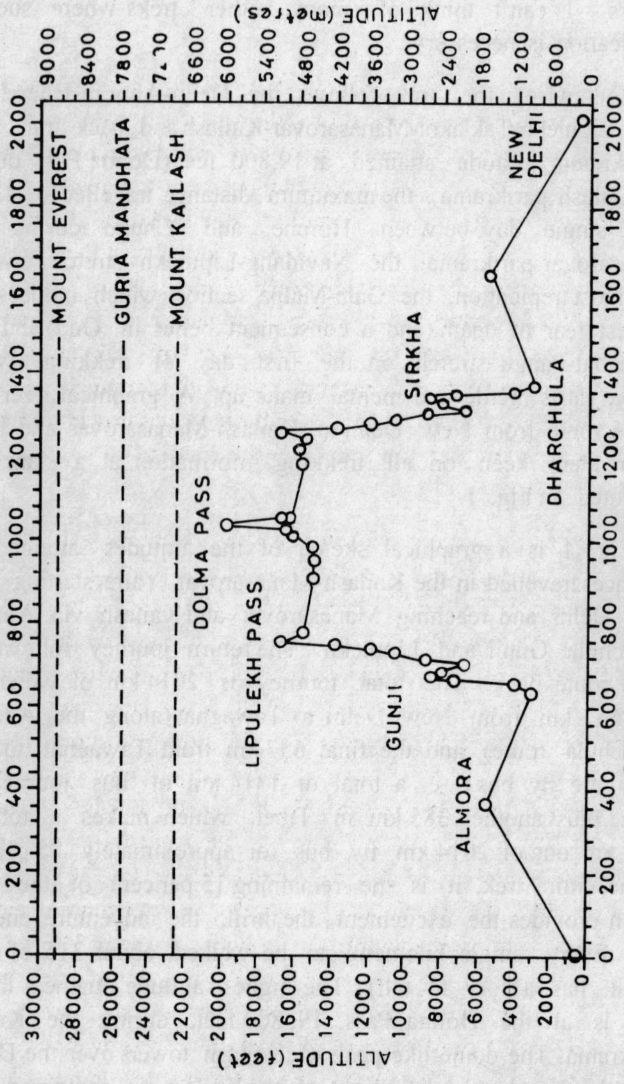


*Fig. 1.* **An altitude-distance-trekking route sketch of the Kailash-Manasarovar Yatra, from start to finish.**

location and halting place is marked with a circle, in the sketch. The altitude of every location has been stated both in feet as well as in metres on the vertical left and vertical right of this sketch. The distance of any given location from New Delhi, along the trekking route can also be calculated from this sketch.

**The Trekking Route: A Short Description**

A major portion of the journey to Kailash Manasarovar from Tawaghat is along 2 feet wide paths, continually drenched by rain, and occasionally through waterfalls, with loose, non-basaltic rocky faces on the left bank causing frequent landslides. Precipitous, 2000 feet gorges on the right lead vertically into a turbulently flowing Kaliganga river which flows as if it were taking part in the Indianapolis-500. At some places, the trekking path travels along the Kali embankment and at these adventure points, the Kali's ferocity and turbulence evoke more gasps of amazement than of fear.

The Kaliganga gorge is about 5000 feet deep (about one mile) and matches the Colorado-Grand Canyon system in magnitude and grandeur. However, and this is very unusual indeed, the Kaliganga river which affords a natural border between India and Nepal, has the uncanny knack for looking very tame and docile on film. That it is impossible to make a transverse river crossing, is not evident from about 200 photographs that I have seen or taken on this subject and the river reminds one more of the tame Thames at Tilberry Port than the fiery Narmada at Jabalpur which might be a closer approximation of reality. A few object-oriented photographs have brought out the "washing machine" effect in this river very vividly and are portrayed in an appropriate section of this adventure documentation.

Throughout the trek, the terrain changes continually as ascent progresses. Some exotic flora and fauna are seen at altitudes between 7,000 and 12,000 feet. Colours take on innumerably deeper shades and richer hues than they do in cities like Mumbai. An entire section on Himalayan flowers is featured in the book and surprisingly, many of the breathtaking photographs and foliage have been captured using relatively modest equipment and non-professional accessories. All of us however, must agree on one point: To take good photographs, you don't necessarily need sophisticated and expensive equipment, but you always need an eye for beauty.

In an overview, it is not only Mount Kailash and Lake Manasarovar which are worthy of adventurous worship, no doubt they are the most important, but there are also innumerable other, lesser known sights, fragrances, experiences and evocative memories that make Kailash and Manasarovar more a journey than a destination: it is a communion with yourself, which no package tour operator or adventure club can provide. I believe: *Kailash is a state of Manas* (mind) and this thought is about the most religious that I have had in the compilation of this book.

**Don't go with Statistics. Go with an Attitude**

Approximately 85 per cent of the total distance covered in the Kailash-Manasarovar Yatra, i. e. 1701 km out of 2014 km, is a bus journey and once this fact has dawned upon an amateur trekker, he begins to live under the delusion of being able to overcome whatever difficulties and obstacles the remaining 15 per cent may throw at him. Walking 315 km (about the same as a Mumbai to Pune and back trip, by road) over a period of at least 25 walking days leading to an average of less than 13 km a day shouldn't be much trouble, or so he thinks. What he doesn't know is that the terrain is such that it will take him at least 8 hours (and sometimes even 12) of walking each day to cover his average of 13 km and at the end of 25 days walking, he will have lost close to 20 pounds in weight, could be savagely sun-burnt, will have been exposed to the extreme elements and will have had the daylights scared out of him on more occasions than one. When one treks in the mountains, it is the attitude and outlook which distinguish a good trekker from a dead one. About half the books cited in the bibliography say so and the author with whatever experience he claims to possess, endorses this view. Dewang Norbu, a noted scholar on the Kailash-Manasarovar region says "Seek with humility and you will accomplish". I think this ideology sums it all up. The accompanying sketch in Fig. 2 illustrates and maps out the trekking route in the Kailash- Manasarovar Yatra in terms of altitudes, distances, absolute distances from New Delhi, inclines and gradients during the trek and the number of trekking halts and transit points throughout the trek. In figure a destination-distance-altitude-inclination sketch of the trek to Kailash-Manasarovar has been represented graphically. Most circled points indicate places of night-halt after the day's trekking. The exceptions are Tawaghat (both ways), Lipulekh Pass (both ways), Dolma Pass, Khojarnath, Navidang (while returning) and Pangu (while returning). The altitude of each location in feet and metres is also available. Altitudes above 10,000 feet are classified as high altitudes and those above 15,000 feet as extremely high altitudes. Distances between "trekking segments" can also be known from this figure. The scales on the altitude and distance axes have been so chosen that when the reader follows the trekking path outlined by the line which weaves through the circles, he is able to assess the "level of difficulty" associated with each trekking segment. As a thumb rule, when the line climbs more and spreads less, the route is difficult. Examples are Tawaghat to Pangu *(Thanedar ki Chadhai)*, Malpa to Budhi to Gunji (Chhia Lekh Top), Navidang to Lipulekh, Direbu to Dolma Pass and Taklakot to Lipulekh. Similarly, in the sketch, sharp descents are lines closer to a vertical drop than to a lazy meandering fall. Examples are Gala to Malpa, Lipulekh to Taklakot, Dolma Pass to Zongzerbu, Lipulekh to Navidang, among others. However, difficulty from "river factors" is not measured by this sketch.

Of the 700 km distance from Tawaghat to Tawaghat via the Dolma Pass, certain segments like the Lipulekh-Taklakot (19 km), the Taklakot-Horche (135 km), the Zaidi-Tarchen (30 km) and the Tarchen-Taklakot-Khojarnath-Taklakot-Lipulekh (201 km) sections, i. e., a total of 385 km is by way of a bus journey. The actual trek is over the remaining 700 - 385 = 315 km. Readers keen on a step-by-step Destination- Distance-Altitude account might find the information in Table 1 to be of interest.

## Table 1

A step-by-step Destination-Distance-Altitude account of the Kailash-Manasarovar Yatra. This Table has been accorded a mathematical layout for its utility as a ready-reckoner. A visual display of the information in this Table has been compiled and presented separately in Figs. 1, 2, 17 and 28.

| *Day* | *Place* | *Altitude* | *Mode of Transport* | *Distance* | *Bus Journey* | *Trek (Foot)* |
|---|---|---|---|---|---|---|
| 1. | New Delhi | 400 ft | Own arrangement | 0 km | 0 km | 0 km |
| 2. | Almora | 5400 ft | Bus | 370 km | 370 km | 0 km |
| 3. | Dharchula | 2970 ft | Bus | 270 km | 640 km | 0 km |
| 3(a). | Tawaghat | 3960 ft | Bus | 17 km | 657 km | 0 km |
| 4. | Pangu | 7260 ft | On foot | 9 km | 657 km | 9 km |
| 4(a) | Narayan Ashram | 7820 ft | On foot | 7 km | 657 km | 16 km |
| 5. | Sirkha | 8450 ft | On foot | 5 km | 657 km | 21 km |
| 6. | Gala | 8050 ft | On foot | 16 km | 657 km | 37 km |
| 7. | Malpa | 6765 ft | On foot | 10 km | 657 km | 47 km |
| 8. | Budhi | 8845 ft | On foot | 8 km | 657 km | 55 km |
| 9. | Gunji | 10625 ft | On foot | 18 km | 657 km | 73 km |
| 10. | Kalapani | 11880 ft | On foot | 10 km | 657 km | 83 km |
| 11. | Navidang | 13800 ft | On foot | 9 km | 657 km | 92 km |
| 11(a). | Lipulekh Pass | 16730 ft | On foot | 7 km | 657 km | 99 km |
| 12. | Taklakot | 15500 ft | Bus | 19 km | 676 km | 99 km |
| 13. | Taklakot | 15500 ft | Rest day | 0 km | 676 km | 99 km |

| *Day* | *Place* | *Altitude* | *Mode of Transport* | *Distance* | *Bus Journey* | *Trek (Foot)* |
|---|---|---|---|---|---|---|
| 14. | Taklakot | 15500 ft | Rest day | 0 km | 676 km | 99 km |
| 15. | Horche | 14950 ft | Bus | 135 km | 811 km | 99 km |
| 16. | Chugu | 14950 ft | On foot | 42 km | 811 km | 141 km |
| 17. | Zaidi | 15000 ft | On foot | 32 km | 811 km | 173 km |
| 18. | Zaidi | 15000 ft | Rest day | 0 km | 811 km | 173 km |
| 19. | Tarchen | 16200 ft | Bus/Truck | 32 km | 843 km | 173 km |
| 20. | Direbu | 16500 ft | On foot | 14 km | 843 km | 187 km |
| 20(a) | Dolma Pass | 19800 ft | On foot | 6 km | 843 km | 193 km |
| 21. | Zongzerbu | 16500 ft | On foot | 13 km | 843 km | 206 km |
| 22. | Tarchen | 16200 ft | On foot | 12 km | 843 km | 218 km |
| 23. | Taklakot | 15500 ft | Bus | 130 km | 973 km | 218 km |
| 24. | Taklakot | 15500 ft | Bus to Khojarnath | 52 km | 1025 km | 218 km |
| 24(a). | Lipulekh Pass | 16730 ft | Mainly bus | 19 km | 1044 km | 218 km |
| 24(b). | Navidang | 13800 ft | On foot | 7 km | 1044 km | 225 km |
| 25. | Kalapani | 11880 ft | On foot | 9 km | 1044 km | 234 km |
| 26. | Gunji | 10625 ft | On foot | 10 km | 1044 km | 244 km |
| 27. | Budhi | 8845 ft | On foot | 18 km | 1044 km | 262 km |
| 27(a) | Malpa | 6765 ft | On foot | 8 km | 1044 km | 270 km |
| 28. | Gala | 8050 ft | On foot | 10 km | 1044 km | 280 km |
| 29. | Sirkha | 8450 ft | On foot | 16 km | 1044 km | 296 km |

| Day | Place | Altitude | Mode of Transport | Distance | Bus Journey | Trek (Foot) |
|---|---|---|---|---|---|---|
| 29(a) | Pangu | 7260 ft | On foot | 8 km | 1044 km | 304 km |
| 29(b) | Tawaghat | 3960 ft | On foot | 9 km | 1044 km | 313 km |
| 30. | Dharchula | 2970 ft | Bus | 17 km | 1061 km | 313 km |
| 31. | Almora | 5400 ft | Bus | 270 km | 1331 km | 313 km |
| 32. | New Delhi | 400 ft | Bus | 370 km | 1701 km | 313 km |
| **End of Trek** | | | **Total Distance** | **2014 km** | **2014 km** | |

***Note :*** All altitudes are accurate to within 50 feet of the values stated in this Table. However, from previous documentation, the altitudes of Taklakot and Dolma Pass have been noticed to vary by unusually huge amounts, often upto 2000 feet for the same location. Different authors quote different altitudes for Taklakot and Dolma Pass and it is difficult to determine which values are measured and which values are borrowed from literature. Most of the altitude figures in this book have been quoted from Swami Pranavananda's research. One reason for the discrepancy in altitude figures might be due to the difference in nomenclature. While some places are measured for height above Mean Sea Level, others are measured in terms of an elevation above River Level (The Indus in this case). Strictly speaking, the latter is a very loose concept considering that localised river basins in the mountains are seldom horizontally planar.

**Tangible Gains from a Trek to Kailash-Manasarovar**

What does an amateur trekker gain from a trek to Kailash-Manasarovar? Well, whatever he gains is something very solid and useful. He cannot wear it. He cannot drive it to the office. He cannot spend it. But he can feel it. And live with it. And remember it. And cherish it. It will have been an extremely moving experience in adventure. And he will want to go back to the same place for more. And more. And still more, just as I do. The object being to seek, to improvise, to innovate, to research and to learn. Isn't that gain enough?

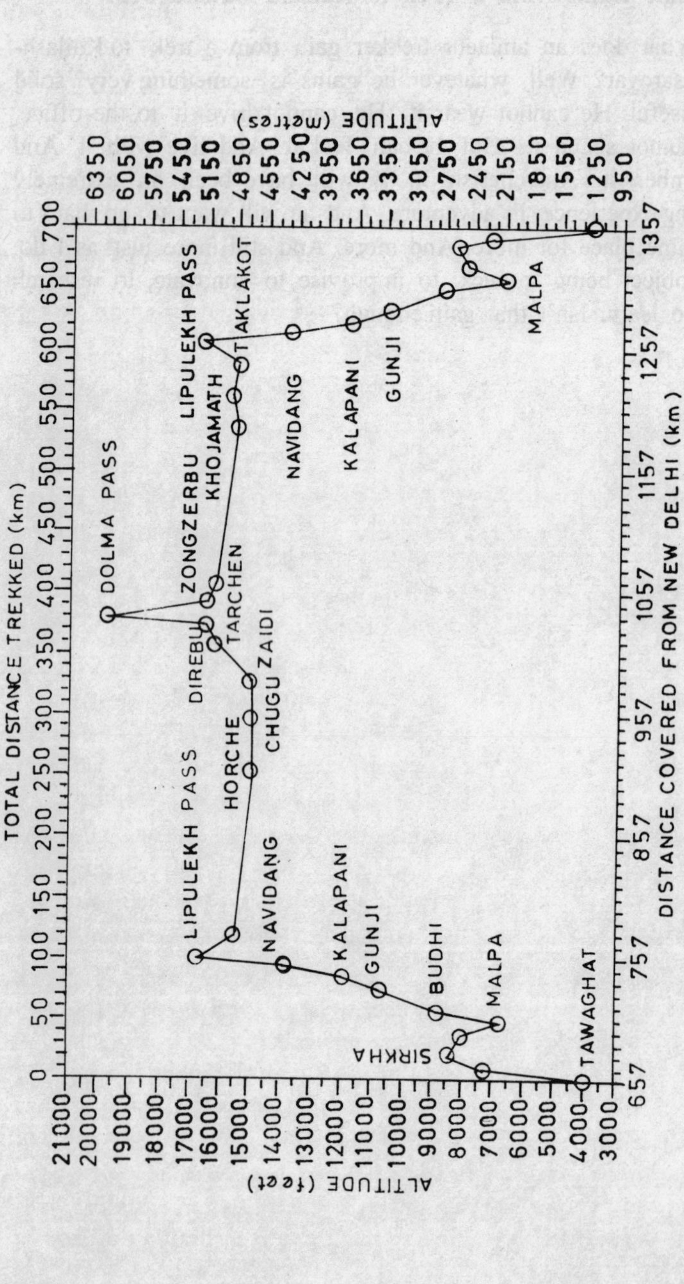


*Fig. 2.* **A Destination-Distance-Altitude-Inclination sketch of the trekking route to Kailash-Manasarovar.**

# 2

# Adventure in the Kailash-Manasarovar Region: Theory and Practice

Kailash and Manasarovar or Kang-Rinpoche and Mapam Tso, as they are respectively and respectfully known in Tibet, have been known to Indian traders for several centuries, as small, yet picturesque detours along the Indo-Tibetan trade routes. From Swami Pranavananda's historical tracings, there are at least a dozen more routes leading to Kailash: one from Ladakh, another from Srinagar, a third, undocumented one from Kedarnath, another from western Uttar Pradesh, still another from upper Assam and several more non-permanent, fair weather tracks and trails all culminating into a circle of roughly 100 km diameter with Taklakot and Gartok forming diametrically opposite ends. It is along these trade routes that alternatives to the presently followed Dharchula-Lipulekh route exist. Detailed information on the alternative trekking routes to Kailash-Manasarovar for readers interested in geography, is presented in Table 2.

## Routes to Kailash-Manasarovar from India

At least twelve trekking routes to Kailash-Manasarovar from India, are known to exist. Each of these routes lies along one of three main trekking corridors: the Lipulekh-Gurla Mandhata corridor, the Ladakh-Gartok corridor and the Lhasa-Tirthapuri corridor. The three corridors meet near the town of Parkha situated at the centroid of the Kailash-Manasarovar-Rakshas Tal triangle. The region can be approached from the south-west (along the Lipulekh-Gurla Mandhata corridor) in which case the trekker comes to Manasarovar (Zaidi) first and then proceeds to

**Table 2**

Different routes to Kailash and Manasarovar from India. Roughly, three different directional approaches are known. The region can be approached from the south-west (along the Lipulekh Pass) in which case the trekker comes to Manasarovar (Zaidi) first and then proceeds to Kailash (Tarchen). Another route is from the north-west (Simla or Srinagar-Ladakh) in which case, the trekker comes first to Tarchen (along the Rakshas Tal, in one case) and then reaches Parkha and Horche. The third variation is an eastward arrival from Lhasa, reaching Manasarovar at Horche and proceeding to Tarchen via Parkha. Several fair-weather, non-permanent routes to Tarchen arriving from the north also exist. These are perhaps the most difficult, and typically traverse portions along the Takla Makan and Gobi deserts, upstream the Indus for a major distance and adopt an extremely circuitous trail to avoid a transverse desert crossing. The routes have been used mainly by Russian and Mongol explorers and expeditions from Kyrgyzstan, Kazakhstan and other places and generally follow the Yarkand-Gartok trekking lane. Russians explorers have made the Kailash-Manasarovar region the focus of their research for the last hundred years or so, even before the times of Dr. Sven Hedin and an extremely huge inventory of scientific information on the region is available in Russian which would perhaps make a very interesting object of study.

| *Route* | *Start From* | *End At* | *Important Stopovers* | *Highest Point* | *One Way Distance* |
|---|---|---|---|---|---|
| 1. | Almora | Tarchen | Almora, Berinag, Askot, Dharchula, Khela, Pangu, Gunji, Kalapani Lipu Lekh, Taklakot, Manasarovar, Ganga Chhu, Tarchen. | Lipulekh Pass (16,730 feet, windswept, snow capped, must be crossed before sun gets high) | 381 km |
| 2. | Almora | Tarchen | Almora, Berinag, Askot, Dharchula, Khela, Dar, Nagaling. Go, Dave, Darma Pass, Mangul, Lama-chhorten, Chakra mandi, Chhumik-shala, Tarchen. | Darma Pass (18,510 feet, deceitful crevasses on and alongside the pass) | 363 km |

*Fig. 11.*

*Fig. 12.*

*Fig. 13.*

*Fig. 15.*

*Fig. 16.*

| *Route* | *Start From* | *End At* | *Important Stopovers* | *Highest Point* | *One Way Distance* |
|---|---|---|---|---|---|
| 3. | Almora | Tarchen | Almora, Bageshwar, Milam, Dhunga, Unta-Dhura Pass, Jayanti Pass, Kungri-Bingri Pass, Chhirchin, Thajang, Gyanima Mandi, Chhumik-shala, Tarchen. | Jayanti Pass (18,500 feet, very steep ascent for about 5 km) | 336 km |
| 4. | Joshimath | Tarchen | Joshimath, Suraitota, Malari, Niti, Guthing, Khyunglung, Niti Pass, Changlus, Nabra Mandi, Sibchilim Mandi, Gyanima Mandi, Chhumik-shala, Tarchen. | Niti Pass (16,600 feet, last 3 km is an extremely steep ascent, Indian boundary, Kailash seen from here) | 320 km |
| 5. | Joshimath | Tarchen | Joshimath, Suraitota, Malari, Niti, Damjan, Damjan-Niti Pass, Hoti, Chhalampa, Sibchilim Mandi, Gyanima Mandi, Chhumik-shala, Tarchen. | Damjan-Niti Pass (16,200 feet, Kailash seen from here) | 256 km |
| 6. | Joshimath | Tarchen | Joshimath, Suraitota, Malari, Timarsim, Kalazabar, Hoti-Niti Pass, Hoti, Chhalampa Sibchilim Mandi, Gyanima Mandi, Chhumik-shala, Tarchen. | Hoti-Niti Pass (16,390 feet, negotiable ascent, but very steep descent) | 253 km |
| 7. | Badrinath | Tarchen | Badrinath, Ghastoli, Sarasvati, Mana Pass, Poti, Jogorav, Ramurav, Thhuling Gompa, Mangang, Dapa, Nabra Mandi, Sibchilim Mandi, Gyanima Mandi, Chhumik-shala, Tarchen. | Mana Pass (18,400 feet) | 381 km |
| 8. | Gangotri | Tarchen | Gangotri, Nilang, Dusundu, Tipani, Mandi, Jelukhaga Pass, Puling Mandi, Sharvarao, Thhuling, Mangang, Dapa, Nabra Mandi, Sibchilim Mandi, Gyanima Mandi, Chhumik-shala, Tarchen. | Jelukhaga Pass (also called Tsagchhok la, 17,490 feet, Indian boundary) | 389 km |

| *Route* | *Start From* | *End At* | *Important Stopovers* | *Highest Point* | *One Way Distance* |
|---|---|---|---|---|---|
| 9. | Simla | Tarchen | Simla, Narkanda, Rampur, Nichar, Poo, Shipki Pass, Khiniphuk, Shangtsi Zong. Gartok, Missar Tasam, Tirthapuri, Tarchen. | Path almost traces the Sutlej upstream. Shipki Pass (15,400 feet) | 701 km |
| 10. | Simla | Tarchen | Simla, Narkanda, Rampur, Nichar, Poo, Shipki Pass, Khiniphuk, Tibu, Thhuling, Mangang, Dapa, Nabra Mandi, Sibchilim Mandi, Gyanima Mandi, Chhumik-shala, Tarchen. | Shipki Pass (15,400 feet) | 757 km |
| 11. | Srinagar | Tarchen | Srinagar, Sonmarg, Zoji la, Kargil, Leh, Upshi, Taglang la, Langsham, Demchhok, Tashigong, Langmar, Gargunsa, Gartok, Missar Tasam, Tirthapuri, Tarchen. | Path almost traces the Indus upstream. Taglang la (17,500 feet). Long route but historically significant, proposed to be reopened from Leh onwards. | 957 km |
| 12. | Lhasa | Tarchen | Lhasa, Ralung, Gyantse, Shigartse Saka Zong, Tradum, Tuksum, Tamsang, Thokchen, Parkha, Tarchen. | All along the Tibetan Plateau. Ralung (14,700 feet) and Tarchen (16,200 feet) are the high points. This route and variations thereabout, from Kathmandu, has been opened to private tour operators. | Approx. 1280 km along the present Lhasa-Kara-koram highway. |

Kailash (Tarchen). Another route traces from the north-west direction (Ladakh-Gartok corridor) in which case, the trekker comes first to Tarchen (along the Rakshas Tal, in one case) and then reaches Parkha and Horche. The third variation is an eastward arrival from Lhasa, reaching Manasarovar at Horche and proceeding to Tarchen via Parkha (Lhasa-Tirthapuri corridor). The Ministry of External Affairs organised Kailash-Manasarovar Yatra follows the Lipulekh- Gurla Mandhata corridor. Organised and conducted tours are permitted only along the Lhasa-Tirthapuri corridor which involve a transport by bus or Land Rovers or Land Cruisers or Pajeros over the Tibetan Plateau. Presently, and for the last few decades as well, the Ladakh-Gartok corridor has been closed for trekking though, as recently as in April 1997, a proposal has been mooted by the Jammu and Kashmir Tourism Department to open up this trekking route. Out of a sheer fascination for the mountains and high altitude trekking along newer and newer mountain trails, the author has offered his services to the Government to form part of the first exploratory team along the proposed route to Gartok. The Government's response is awaited with great anticipation.

**Routes to Kailash-Manasarovar from the far North**

Several fair-weather, non-permanent routes to Tarchen arriving from the north also exist. These are perhaps the most difficult, and typically traverse portions along the Takla Makan and Gobi deserts, upstream the Indus for a major distance and adopt an extremely circuitous trail to avoid a transverse desert crossing. The routes have been used mainly by Russian and Mongol explorers and expeditions from Kyrgyzstan, Kazakhstan and other places and generally follow the Yarkand-Gartok trekking lane. Russians explorers have made the Kailash-Manasarovar region the focus of their research for the last hundred years or more, much before the times of Dr. Sven Hedin, and an extremely huge inventory of scientific information on the region is available in the Russian language which would perhaps make a very interesting object of study.

## The Absence of Informative Trekking Maps on the Region

A few preliminary sketches of some trekking routes along the Aksai Chin have been compiled by Lieutenant C. J. Otto Kjelstrom in 1908, for Dr. Sven Hedin, and have been documented in his treatise. The quality of drawings and tracings has perhaps not been reproduced faithfully in print and as a result, much ambiguity prevails on trekking distances and paths along geographic Mercators. The Oxford School Atlas too, does not do adequate justice in mapping out the "fuller" projections and physical features of the region. An accurate geographical map of the region is very scarce to come by and might prove to be an interesting area of work to amateur and professional cartographers. Present day maps invariably represent the Kailash-Manasarovar region as a curved surface, making distance and spread estimates difficult. The author recalls seeing a very good geophysical map of the terrain at the Seralung Gompa during the Manasarovar parikrama. Due to the inaccessibility of GT maps and other visual aids to the general trekking public, crude, yet accurate sketches, even at a small geographic scale, might ultimately lead to the development of a trekking map based on ascertained measurements and marked positions. Mountaineers and potential Kailash-Manasarovar trekkers have a positive obligation to fulfil in case the region is to come out of its state of "geographic neglect".

## Kailash-Manasarovar along the Lipulekh-Gurla Mandhata Corridor

The Kailash-Manasarovar trekking route followed by the author was the Almora-Tarchen route along the Lipulekh- Gurla Mandhata corridor. A motor transport was available from Almora to Tawaghat. Trekking began from Tawaghat and progressed approximately north-eastwards. Trekkers reached Manasarovar first (at Zaidi) and Kailash subsequently (at Tarchen). The return journey retraced the onward journey along the Gurla Mandhata-Lipulekh direction i.e. along Route No. 1 in Table 2.

This book is a description of trekking experiences from Tawaghat to Tawaghat via Lipulekh, Taklakot, Zaidi and Tarchen.

## Planning the Trek upto a 10,000 Feet Altitude (Delhi to Gunji)

After responding to the press advertisement in March and getting an acknowledgement in April, there was nothing to do until a sudden selection telegram for Batch 5 arrived in early June. "Ah Great!" was the typical response "I hope I can do it. Let me see if my insurance premia are all paid up". "What about my leave? Do I have enough cash? What things will I need in my trekking and travel kit? I haven't got my medical tests and reports ready yet. When do I pack? There is so much work to do, in the office and at home. I have to reach Delhi in 15 days and prepare to be away for about 45 days. And now that I have been selected, should I really go"? These are some questions which bother everybody.

## Administrative Protocols

Fifteen days later, most of the people who got the telegram have reported at the hotel specified in New Delhi. Drop-outs are few. Everyone is charged with excitement and anticipation. We receive instructions from the Ministry of External Affairs that the next day everyone will be taken to South Block for some briefing.

On the next day, payments to KMVN and submission of passports and indemnity bonds to the Ministry staff were attended to. The jobs were completed by noon and the yatris were brought back to their hotel. After lunch, some yatris felt their kit was incomplete and thought it prudent to make a few purchases in Delhi. Earlier in the day, it was decided that a common food parcel providing for eight days for everyone would be compiled. I think this was a good decision to take. The parcel also included a few pots and pans. Two men within the group were appointed Luggage Officers to oversee and ensure the safe transport of everybody's luggage for all of the next 35 days. This is one of the greatest responsibilities that one could be saddled with. As a result, a Luggage Officer must be one who can keep track and maintain good mental records.

The next day, the yatris were taken to the ITBP Hospital for medical checks and an examination of test reports. Even the slightest signs of a high blood pressure or a high glucose in blood would mean failure and a consequent cancellation of the trip for that individual. One, person in our group failed, and two were declared a border-line pass. They were always to be under the close scrutiny of Mr. Satish Kumar, our Liaison Officer.

The third day was scheduled for issuance of the Chinese visa and collecting foreign exchange. The visa was a group visa, with no endorsement on the passport. It was a simple list of all the yatris which was certified and stamped by the consulate. A maximum of $ 650 in foreign exchange was made available to each yatri. Of this amount, $ 500 would be paid to the Chinese authority in Taklakot for making basic arrangements. The rest would be used for hiring yaks or ponies and purchase of trinkets in Tibet. Everyone was advised to wind up early that day. The next day, the bus would arrive at 3.00 a.m. so as to leave by 4.00 a.m. and reach Almora, 370 km away, by 6.00 p.m.

**New Delhi to Almora**

The bus left at 4.00 a.m. sharp. The Luggage Officers had a tough time keeping an account of and an eye on every piece of luggage. To provide an indication, for our group of 28, the items not carried on person numbered 63 and weighed 842 kg (as we were to find out at Dharchula). As a result, the group, which had a free allowance of 25 kg per person had to pay for the excess weight at the approximate mule transport rate of 18 paise per kilogram per kilometre. The excess amount was shared equally and in any case, did not amount to much.

The bus sped out of Delhi, crossed the Yamuna and headed towards Almora. The roads were in good shape and empty. A good speed could be gathered. The bus suspension was excellent. Many were lulled into a sleep due to a gentle swaying motion, while others preferred to look out of the window. We were to discover very quickly, that the driver was fond of modern Hindi music played at the maximum blare. His fancy and loud entertainment ideas were quickly stamped out. We were beginning to enjoy ourselves.

We crossed the Ganga, 105 km from Delhi at Gajraula where we stopped for breakfast. We were quite on time. Breakfast consisted of *puris* and *sabji* and at about 6.30 a.m., the bus left Gajraula. The next halt was to be Rampur where we would briefly stop for a welcome by the trading community and for some light snacks. The people were warm and hospitable. By now, it was quite obvious and this thought was to be reinforced time and again that a Kailash-Manasarovar Yatri was a special kind of a person who gained easy acceptance at every place right upto the Indian border town of Navidang.

We reached Bhowali in time for a late lunch. There was hardly a third activity to sitting in the bus and getting down from it at meal times. The bus left Bhowali for Almora by about 2.00 p.m. The terrain was beginning to get quite likeable by now. An ascent had begun and the bus speed had reduced. Cliffs came closer to the roads and bends approached hairpin dimensions. There was a small accident in our group a little before Almora. From the window seat, a gentleman's elbow grazed against the mountain and he went into trauma. The fracture was nasty. Before the close of the first day's travel, we had had an injury. The general euphoria dipped. For the injured, the trek was ruled out. He was sent back to Delhi the next day with an escort.

Anyway, coming back to the subject at hand, we reached the KMVN rest house at Almora at about 5.30 p.m. On Almora, the Uttarakhand tourist department, in its publicity brochure, calls it an *unspoiled child of nature,* but the question of upbringing apart, Almora has a very salubrious and healthy air about it. The town is perched on a 5 km long horse saddle shaped ridge at an altitude of 5400 feet. The natural beauty of Almora is greatly enhanced by the Kumaon hills and the snow clad Himalayas which surround it. The facilities at the rest house were unexpectedly good. Towards 6.30 p.m, the local press came to meet the yatris and give them a little press coverage. Many of us were getting a little irritated at the dignitary status that was being accorded to our group. But the simple hill folk don't look at it that way. For them, it is just part of good hospitality. The flora at the KMVN rest house is quite impressive. We had a quick dinner and retired to our rooms. The rooms had no fans. There was no need for them in any case. It is quite cold even in the summers and blankets were quite necessary. We were to leave for Dharchula at 6.30 a.m. the next day.

**Almora to Dharchula**

The Almora to Dharchula bus route is a continuous up and down from one mountain to another. The bus speed averages to about 25 kmph and the 270 km distance took us about 12 hours.

After an hour's travel from Almora, we stopped at the Golu temple, on the outskirts of Almora. Lord Golu is a Mountain God of Health and Justice and the temple is adorned with hundreds and thousands of metallic bells, in different sizes, shapes and tunes, each symbolic of a thanksgiving. The temple architecture is unique and the very prospect of visiting a temple, ostensibly one of a kind, should hold an attraction even for those who are not very devout.

Another halt was taken a few hours later at the Kainchi temple which was scrupulously clean and well looked after. The temple is located on the other side of a picturesque rivulet and the summer flowers in full bloom provide for good photography.

Lunch was taken at Chaukori, which is an important KMVN destination. It was raining heavily by the time we reached Chaukori. The rains kept up their tempo until well past 2.00 p.m. Lunch was a simple but filling affair and the brief rains, cloud cover. winds and the chill put together a very romantic setting. The rest house also has provision for mountain-cycling and has a rolling stock of about 25 well maintained mountain cycles. It was fun cycling up and down the local hills in and around Chaukori in the interval between lunch and departure for Dharchula.

The bus left for Dharchula at about 3.00 p.m. Visibility was poor in view of the rains and progress was slow. It was great fun sitting at the window watching the hills and rivers rush past while an occasional water drop fell on your spectacle rim. There was only one thought running through each mind: 'Tomorrow we start trekking, the next few weeks are going to be tough, I hope I can make it successfully'. Looking back at that stage, well everybody returned safely from the trek, but there is no escaping the uneasiness that one feels on approaching Dharchula. Even people who have completed the Kailash-Manasarovar circuit on earlier occasions, admit to 'butterflies in the stomach' on approaching Dharchula.

The night halt was scheduled at the KMVN Rest House at Dharchula where the tourist bus reached at about 6.00 p.m. Dharchula is a unique town of sorts. It is the final town in this part of India where a citizen can go on his own free will. Regions beyond Dharchula are militarily sensitive and access is restricted to people on legitimate work. Permissions from the District Magistrate are necessary for all forays into the "zero-area" as it is called. Of course, if the trekker is on the Kailash-Manasarovar Yatra organised by the Ministry of External Affairs, the government arranges for all permissions without most of the trekkers even knowing that such a permit needs to be issued. A new development which occurred in Government circles in Dharchula at that time, was the issuance of Indo-Tibet trade licences, on a yearly basis, at a nominal fee. The trade licences are valid upto the Tibetan town of Taklakot and merchants usually carry coffee and groundnuts into Tibet. Merchandise is laden on ponies or mules and the caravan undertakes the high-altitude trade sojourn into Tibet, under the eagle eye of the Indo-Tibetan Border Police, under inhospitable conditions of temperature, wind, rain, snow and terrain. Frequently, men, beast and trade-ware are lost to the ferocious river. In addition, the author is quite convinced that profit margins in the trans-Himalayan trade do not outweigh the risks and difficulties. Surprisingly, just like all expeditions since the time of Marco Polo, trade continues essentially because the traders, many of whom are in their early twenties, love their mountains and prefer their adventure in unadulterated form. To be a little honest with his readers, the author is quite serious on acquiring a trade license to avail of unlimited trips to the high altitude area, if the government will allow him, that is?

But coming back to where we are, at Dharchula that is, there are two Dharchulas: one in India, the other in Nepal, both 200 metres apart, with the Kaliganga river separating them. You may cross over from the Indian Dharchula to the Nepali Dharchula using the quaint little bridge which gently sways with the wind. The bridge remains open from sunrise to sunset, and though there are a few formal customs checkposts on either side of the international border, actual scrutiny is seldom required and even lesser done. Yatris generally go over to Nepal to purchase trinkets more for the record of having bought something from across the border than for anything else. The Nepali settlement is quite small and seems to specialise in rubber shoes only in sizes five and six. There is a Kathmandu International Cafe which is a roadside watering hole where only tea is available. I didn't find it worthwhile buying anything here; to me the place resembled an extended version of Mumbai's Lohar Chawl. However, in case you wish to make a telephone call to your near and dear, it is quicker and better to make an ISD call from the Nepali Dharchula than to make an STD from the Indian Dharchula from where connections take very long to establish.

Dharchula also has a rickety cinema hall and taking in a movie, local style on your return from Kailash-Manasarovar might be good proposition. The town has a sizeable Muslim population and beyond Dharchula you rarely come across any followers of Islam, though you do meet a few Christians in and around the Tibetan town of Taklakot.

Dharchula is also the Porters' Headquarters. All porters and ponymen who wish to offer their services into the zero area are registered here. Records are strictly and scrupulously maintained, but then, such a task is not so difficult either; in small towns such as Dharchula, everyone knows everyone else. Porters may be hired at Rs. 90 per day and a good porter will also run errands for you and even wash your clothes when you finish with the day's trekking. Ponymen, however, are a law onto themselves. They will only transport you from one point to another and additionally, their horses are available only during the ascent and not while descending. What's more your ponyman will not allow your friend to use your horse even when you choose to walk. Lease is not transferable. But there is an easy way out. Assuming that you do hire a pony at Rs. 175 per day, please do insist that you collect the ponyman's service pass. Retain the pass with you until you don't need his services any more. The ponyman knows you could report him to the authorities and recommend cancellation of his service pass. Such a step usually ensures a better service.

## Dharchula to Tawaghat

The 17 km stretch between Dharchula and Tawaghat, traversed by bus, is one of great anticipation and some trepidation. By now, it has just about sunk in into the trekker's mind that whatever his background, the next several days are going to be vastly different from whatever he has seen or experienced before. Naturally, this common fear of the unknown draws people closer and people begin to open up a little. There is a grim, resolute expression on each face as the bus speeds towards Tawaghat.

Prior to departure from Dharchula, the luggage belonging to each batch is weighed on a huge arm balance at the KMVN Rest House. Each yatri may carry upto 25 kg, however luggage allowances may be pooled. A small payment is charged for excess weight. All luggage pieces are mounted on ponies with about four items to a pony. The luggage is covered with plastic sheets and finally with jute sacks and tied with nylon ropes to protect their contents from rains, dust and falling rocks and gravel. It is important that a prospective trekker pack his material in soft rucksacks so as to make the piece amenable to bending and twisting during transport. Hard tops and suitcases should not be carried. Ideally, each trekker should line the innards of his luggage with a thick polyethylene sheet and pack the item in a nylon sack (the kind used to pack fertilisers). Each piece should be labelled and tied with a strong nylon rope. Do not pack your cameras, optical instruments, ham radios and similar material into your rucksacks. The luggage for transport by ponies is handled in a very rough manner. Additionally, overhanging cliffs or jutting rocks may rip off a few luggage pieces and a few items might spill out, get lost or get stolen. Once the luggage is laden on the ponies, it is practically untraceable until the end of the day's trek, so keep the necessities with you in a small sling bag or better, in a haversack so as to keep your hands free. The contents of the haversack which must be updated from the pony luggage everyday, must essentially include a water-bottle, some light snacks, a packet of glucose and some electrolytes, a small towel, a raincoat, an extra pair of shoes and socks in case the ones in use get drenched, a torch, a roll of tissues and a pair of sunglasses. Never keep your passport, foreign exchange or camera in any bag. Carry them on your person and a waist-wallet might be a useful hold-all for these items.

As regards distribution of luggage, some yatris hardly carry any luggage at all, their kit consists essentially of some fancy camera equipment and an odd video camera or so, and the bare minimum in clothing and necessities. Others travel as if they were permanently relocating to Kailash, complete with pressure cookers, portable gas cylinders and microwave ovens. If I were to recommend a 35-day Kailash travel kit, I would follow the Ministry of External Affairs' guidelines strictly to the letter in all categories except food. Yatris tend to carry enough food to feed an army. They pay luggage charges for transport of their rations, most of which they cannot consume and finally, on their return to Dharchula after 30 days of trekking, they donate left-overs in return for good services received. To calculate how much you are really going to need, I will provide you with a good rule of thumb. The only occasions when food needs to be cooked on your own are in the three days of the Kailash parikrama, one rest day at Tarchen, two days during the Manasarovar parikrama and one rest day at Zaidi which makes a total of seven days. I would suggest that each person carry four days ration and stretch them on to seven days. One doesn't feel much hungry at high altitudes. Carry plenty of electrolytes and glucose sachets in any case; dehydration can be severe. A sun-screen moisturiser might also be handy. The sun beats down heavily during the Manasarovar parikrama and sun burns can be oppressive.

**Tawaghat to Pangu**

I think I should begin this paragraph with a note of caution for anyone who is proud of his "walking skills". The mountains are hardly the sort of place to indulge in bravado or show-off. To illustrate the point I am trying to make: Tawaghat to Pangu is a 9 km stretch, of which the last 3 km are along an absolutely flat table-top. So where is the problem? The real McCoy is in the first 6 km in which you ascend from 3960 feet to 7160 feet, which translates into a vertical rise of one km. A slope of 1 in 6 is staggeringly huge and just for the sake of continuing the mathematics a little further, corresponds to an inclination of about 10 degrees. Most trucks would have to drive in the first gear and it doesn't really make sound trekking sense to start bolting for Pangu the moment the team is flagged off at Tawaghat. Relax buddy, Kailash is more a journey than a destination and the Holy mountain is not running away anywhere, it plans to stay exactly where it has been for the last several centuries. So take it easy and try not to gasp for breath and consequently fill your lungs with water – you could land yourself into some serious trouble otherwise. Believe me, though I covered the distance in three hours, most took four and some took even five. I decided to drop my speed later on, shoot some fancy pictures, take time to smell the flowers, talk to the people living in the hills, watch little children play cricket on whatever flat piece of land they could find, scribble a 15 paise postcard to my boss whilst sitting on a 2-tonne boulder, inspect the numerous steatite and mica deposits as if I were prospecting for gold and do exactly what my adventurous heart fancied.

The Tawalghat to Pangu trek can be very taxing. However, from Tawaghat, a fair weather 20 km motorable detour to Pangu and upto Narayan Ashram, shown along the left bank of the river, exists and is currently in the process of being made into an all weather road. In Fig. 3 observe the force and volume of the water flow, the height of the bridge above the water line, the sedimentary rock deposits on the left river bank and the steep incline that leads to Pangu.

The Tawaghat-Pangu stretch is memorable in more ways than one, for it is here that the first and closest contact with a group just returning from Kailash-Manasarovar is made. The trekkers in Fig. 4 seen descending the *Thanedar ki Chadhai* belong to an earlier group. A few misty clouds can be seen rising into the late morning sky. Descents are perhaps more difficult than ascents for you additionally need to balance and manoeuvre yourself while descending. A 6 feet long, slender stick may sometimes prove handy. The Himalayan non-basaltic mountain soils erode easily. Landslides, such as those shown in this figure get more common, as rains and winds increase in intensity.

But coming back to matters at hand, there is nothing quite as invigorating as a chilled lemonade after a stiff climb. The mountain air is refreshing and provided one walks at a steady pace he does not perspire. Speaking in the same spirit, I think with the proper attitude and frame of mind, one could go on walking endlessly without really feeling drained out. Breathing well, and in good rhythm is the key to a good trekking experience. One does not feel the need to catch in on an afternoon nap while in the mountains and local old wives' tales regard afternoon sleeping to be dangerous. So avoid it at all costs, even if you consider it necessary.

The KMVN Rest House at Pangu is just like any other rest house. It overlooks a valley over which you can study the next day's trekking route. Towards the late evening, rays from the setting sun are reflected by a large mica deposit adjacent to the rest house and would have made for some unusual photographs had I got everything in readiness. By the time my lenses and stands were ready, the light had faded. This leads us to Lesson Number 1 in photography: *Good scenes don't wait for you, you have to wait in readiness for them.*

**Pangu to Sirkha via Narayan Ashram**

The Pangu to Sirkha stretch is about 8 km but if the yatris

wish to visit the Narayan Ashram, a 4 km detour is necessary. In case the trekkers decide to reach Sirkha via Narayan Ashram, it is best that they plan to reach the Ashram by 8.00 a.m. to catch the morning sunrays on the snow clad peaks in nearby Nepal and catch the flowers in the act of blooming, in which case, they must leave Pangu before 6.00 a.m. And this is exactly what our group did. We started the day at a little before 5.00 and departed from Pangu at 5.30 after a quick and light breakfast and hit the hilly track down the mountain. Narayan Ashram lies on a different hill altogether and Sirkha is located on yet another, so there is a continuous descent and ascent in this section of the trek. The descent from Pangu was sharp and necessitated a detour to enable a river crossing. After the river crossing, the trekking route took on an ascent right upto the Narayan Ashram. The village of Sosa is situated somewhere in the middle of the upward journey and roughly on the same altitude as Pangu. The stones of this region were essentially from the calcium carbonate, magnesium carbonate and marble family and the author took time off from his trekking to collect mineralogical samples. Sosa to Narayan Ashram was a steady climb and the terrain was marked with a soil noticeably red in appearance. The trekking path was fairly wide almost throughout the Pangu to Narayan Ashram route and the journey was not as hazardous as a few other sections. In fact, the dense greenery, foliage and bird sounds along the trekking route gave the impression of the trek being a forest walk. Nevertheless, this section of the trek was novel and quite enjoyable. The Narayan Ashram is situated on a plateau shaped like a 18-hole golf course. The course is beautifully landscaped to the extent that its beauty strikes one as being out of the ordinary. The yatris reached the Narayan Ashram by about 8.00 a.m. and stayed there until 11.30 a.m. clicking photographs, watching the mountains, praying in the temple, listening to Swami Tadroopananda's sermons or quite simply taking a stroll in the immediate vicinity of the Ashram. To talk about the Narayan Ashram in brief, the Ashram was founded in 1936 by Shri Narayan Swami at a beautiful location overlooking the Kaliganga at an altitude of about 9,000 feet. The Ashram is a very good place for meditation and houses a prayer hall, a temple dedicated to Lord Vishnu and an extremely well maintained garden. Swami Tadroopananda who is the head priest, is a much accomplished man of a scientific training and an enquiry-based learning. He is also an eloquent speaker and it was refreshing to hear him give a discourse on "A Kailash-Manasarovar Attitude".

The photograph in Fig. 5 shows the main prayer hall at the Narayan Ashram. Seen in the inset is an exquisitely formed idol of Lord Vishnu in artistically carved silverware which lends a halo to the frontispiece. Delicate woodwork and fine, artistic, mesh-like empanelment, as seen on the left and right corners of the sanctum indicate the fineness in art achieved by local artisans even in geographic regimes as distant as these.

The Narayan Ashram to Sirkha section of the trek was quite steep in its ascent, though the descents were gradual. The trekking paths were narrow and strewn with boulders. On the way to Sirkha, some yatris stopped at a village called Sirdang for tea and light refreshments; others who had built up a tempo preferred to walk on. The day's trek ended at Sirkha (8450 feet) on covering 12 km and ascending through about 1190 feet from Pangu (7260 feet).

At the end of the second day's trek, everybody seemed lively and cheerful. Everyone knew that the mental and physical acclimatisation to high altitudes had already begun to take place and that it would only be a matter of time before a steady mountain-walking rhythm was established.

The KMVN Rest House at Sirkha had a nice view of the Annapurnas in Nepal and much time was spent in photography and especially in capturing an elusive rainbow seen after a few light showers towards the late evening. Very far away, on a flat piece of land, almost 1000 feet directly below us, we could see a few children playing cricket with whatever bits of equipment they could quickly assemble. We thought it was remarkable that children living miles away from civilisation made it their business to be well informed on cricketing and sports action. Puran Singh, a local porter, with whom I had got a little friendly, was to tell me that satellite television had made considerable inroads in influencing the social fabric in the villages and MTV was one of the most popular television channels. I was amused at hearing this bit of information. The common folk in India might not be formally educated but they are certainly a well informed, aware and an awakened lot.

From the Sirkha rest house we studied the next day's trekking route which would mainly be down, up, down and flat. The high point of the journey was to be Rungling Top at an altitude of almost 10,000 feet. The next day's trek held promise of great excitement and adventure and everybody was sufficiently motivated. A simple dinner was taken at 8.00 p.m. and by 10.00 p.m. almost everyone was fast asleep. Tomorrow would be another day.

**Sirkha to Gala**

The altitude difference in Sirkha (8450 feet) and Gala (8050 feet) separated over a 16 km distance gives the impression that this trek is a cakewalk, which it is not. Gala lies on a different mountain altogether which is what conceals the catch. As luck would have it, it was raining heavily at night until well past 5.30 in the morning, our scheduled time of departure. When the showers reduced to a drizzle at about 6.00 a.m., our group left Sirkha and descended 400 feet gradually to a small hamlet named Samuri which lies at the foot of the Sirkha hills. The next stage was a difficult 2000 feet climb to Rungling Top (9760 feet). Somewhere in the middle of this ascent lies a one-hut village: Junglechetti, where light refreshments are available from a mountain-man who comes from 20 km away just to earn some clientele on the scheduled Yatra dates. We had a hurried malt drink at Sirkha at the start and a packed *"puri-sabji"* breakfast proved quite handy at Junglechetti. We only wished we had packed some more for we were getting a little hungry by now. Over the last 3-4 days I had made friends with a young teenaged Kumaoni: Puran Singh who was to tell me a great deal about the mountains and trekking short-cuts. I learnt a lot from his association and though I found his short-cuts to be exceedingly dangerous, I was growing to admire his knowledge of the terrain, his simple philosophy of life, if he ever had one, and his firm yet fleet footed trekking technique. I have an impression, Puran Singh could have walked all day without fatigue and arrived at his destination looking as if he had just stepped out of a band box. Puran Singh was a school dropout and made no effort to hide his disdain for formal learning. His belief was that everybody from Mumbai worked in films and until the time we finally parted company, he pestered me no end that I give him a placement in some film-based activity. The admiration for each other was mutual. Incidentally, it was Puran Singh who told me about a monster peak: Panchchula peak, in the vicinity of our trekking route. A perennial cloud cover makes it difficult to estimate heights and buffeting mountain gales had swept off a few climbers a few seasons back.

Rungling Top was the highest point in the trek so far and by the time the group finally got here, many were gasping and preferred to halt for a while to regain their composure. Though the climbing part was over, the descent remained and as we were soon to find out, and remember thereafter, descending is more difficult than climbing for you need to control your momentum at steep gradients and protect your knees from continuous, often violent shocks. We were to learn that descending should take almost as long as climbing up, if it has to be sustained over several days without discomfort. As a thumb rule, a speed of 2.5 km/hr is a good pace to maintain for both climbing and descent on paths, though, it might be a little difficult to maintain this pace for extended time spans.

## Gala to Malpa

Gala to Malpa is a trek which one might call a fun-trail in the adventure sense of the word. The journey is a descent for most of the way and altitude drops from 8050 feet to 6765 feet over a distance of 10 km. A very impressive scenery and river-contact is gained in this section of the trek and the segment provides the first bit of trekking thrill, excitement and adventure in the past few days since trekking began.

The trek started from Gala at about 6.00 a.m. after a light

breakfast. It was just beginning to brighten up at this hour. The trekkers moved along the slightly descending trail and arrived at Jipti, a small village about 1.5 km away, within a quarter of an hour. The next village was Bindakoti, located a further kilometre down the gradual, barely noticeable descent. A few hundred metres away from Bindakoti lies Lakhanpur Top where a small temple has been built. Trekkingwise, Bindakoti is very strategically located. There is an extremely well-conceived short-cut from Bindakoti to Tawaghat via the hill village of Pangla. The short-cut is along a steep hilly descent for a major portion of the way and reduces the trekking duration by about two days. It might be worthwhile to try out this trail on the return journey, as a few of our companions who were in a hurry to get home, had done.

On instructions from the guides, the trekkers decided to wait at Lakhanpur Top until the luggage ponies had overtaken us. Lakhanpur Top to Lakhanpur village, located at the river level, was a sharp descent comprising 4445 stone steps, each about 3 feet wide, 1 foot broad and about 1 foot high. The descent was narrow, with the mountain on one side and the Kaliganga gorge on the other. It was hence necessary that the luggage ponies be sent ahead so that pushing and jostling along narrow paths could be avoided. The 4445 step descent was endless and seemed to last for the better portion of two hours. When the trekkers finally reached Lakhanpur village, they were relieved to note that a small wayside restaurant served hot *parathas* and *sabji*. The hotel location was very prime: overlooking the river as it negotiated a turn in its path, at an altitude of 200 feet above the water level. The river is about 100 feet wide with its bed enjoying a spread of about 300 feet. The turn in the direction of the river flow, in the gorge, is perhaps a matter of interest as the turbulent river carves out a path of shortest distance for itself through the mountains. Erosion due to river effects is very noticeable and prominent and a visual inspection of mountain debris tells us that the area is extremely prone to landslides. We were blissfully unaware that we would be caught in the middle of one such landslide within the next 24 hours.

The trekkers started from Lakhanpur village towards Malpa. The route assumed a slight ascent and ran the river upstream along its right bank. The river roared in the background and its turbulence and impact with the rocks generated a misty spray of water which pleasantly perfumed the trekkers as they trudged along, hardly daring to look at the river during their trek. Nepal lay across on the opposite bank and the sight of a few local rivulets meeting the Kaliganga and contributing to its flow made interesting viewing. Some photographs of a river confluence between Lakhanpur and Najunggarh are presented in this book. As a result of the extremely narrow river gorge, the photograph seems to convey an idea of depth which adds a new perspective photographically, which was not felt in real life.

Fig. 6 shows a panoramic view along the trekking route from Gala to Malpa, midway between Lakhanpur and Najunggarh. The Kaliganga flows from bottom-left to the bottom-right in the photograph. The photograph has been taken from the Indian side and most of the land-mass, forests and greenery seen in the photograph are in Nepal. Tearing down the mountainous gorge from the Nepal side is a local rivulet. The river gorge is at least 1000 feet in depth. A visual inspection of the rocks near the final cascade shows a lateral wear indicative of intense water erosion forces. A few of the rocks near the river bed are likely to be sedimentary in origin. This gorge is enveloped between extremely tall, about 12,000 feet mountains, on practically all sides. As a result, from the waterline, the sky looks like a thin ribbon of blue. The tall mountains make it difficult to have a spatial perception of the sky from the water-front. A wooden bridge over the gorge can be spotted near the slender tree on the right gorge flank. The photograph seems to convey an idea of depth and this is not surprising since the distance between the first cascade and the point of photography is about 800 metres while the gorge is only about 50 metres wide at its mouth. The photograph was taken at about noon-time. The very fact that the fast flowing river takes an almost 90 degree turn in its path after its confluence with the Kaliganga tells the reader of the immense hydrodynamic power that the Kaliganga carries.

Fig. 6 shows a panoramic view of *Najung Jharana* from Najunggarh is shown in Fig. 7. The word 'Jharana' is a misnomer in this case, for this cascading waterfall is no lazily meandering brook, it is much more than poetry in motion It roars incessantly with the valley echoing its every timbre and crescendo. The sound effects at the point of photography are simply overwhelming, possibly more moving than any Dolby Stereo Cinema Sound. The trekkers make a transverse crossing across the waterfall from the left to the right along one of two suspension bridges. The lower one, seen in the photograph, was probably washed away in part, some seasons ago and its woefully twisted and contorted trusses tell a story of the battering it received at the gentle brook's hands. However, the bridge skeleton, though bent out of shape, is surprisingly intact. For a true dare-devil, use of this bridge and its support systems to make the river crossing is strongly recommended, though, the author did not have the gumption to try it himself.

The trail upto Najunggarh continued along the river bank, about 500 feet above the water level. The highlight of the journey upto Najunggarh, is the Najung Jharana.

From Najunggarh, after crossing the Najung Jharana, there exist two trekking routes to Malpa. One climbs steeply into the mountains, is physically demanding to negotiate, but is very safe to traverse. The other cuts through the mountain at a more or less constant elevation above the river, is almost planar until Malpa, but is terribly risky. Very few trekkers actually notice the up-mountain route until they see it descending into Malpa and by default, they end up choosing the riskier, river trail. The river trail is along a route made by blasting the several thousand foot tall mountain, almost at its base, using dynamite. The trekking path is about 2 feet wide and the river on the right hand side looks extremely scary. Additionally, the trekking route takes one through waterfalls which descend down the mountain through 2000 feet vertically. The trail is often from behind the water curtain from left to right and reminds one of Lee Falk's portrayal of the Phantom Skull Cave. The air is electric and the excitement bristles. The 3 km trek to Malpa is completed without a word, essentially because everyone has been awe-struck with the majesty of the untamed wild, tries to get a firm foothold on the cobblestones and is most concerned with his own safety than with taking photographs or indulging in small talk. Besides, the tremendous river noise makes conversation difficult and hearing strained.

When the trekkers reach Malpa they give the impression of having come out of a temple. Expressions are subdued and it takes a while for them to come out of their trance. The rest of the evening is spent in amateur photography and watching the river flow past the rest house. All thoughts on the past and the future are wiped out and only those centered on the present, exist. It is probably felt here first, at Malpa, that Kailash is not a destination but a journey.

**Malpa to Budhi**

The 8 km Malpa to Budhi trekking section is another stiff climb during which the trekker ascends from 6765 feet to 8845 feet over a distance of 8 km. However, as compared to the Tawaghat-Pangu stretch, this segment is much easier due to gradual slopes and lesser risks in view of an increased separation from the river.

About 5 km away from Malpa, downhill most of the way, lies the village of Lamari. The village is situated below a huge mountain wall which towers at least 3000 feet above the village and spreads in the trekking direction for at least 2 km. The first few trekkers on reaching Lamari, were just looking at the mountains, sipping their mountain tea, when it all started.

It was one boulder first which broke loose, gathered momentum and dislodged another in its wake. The dislodging, accumulation and speeding up process built up in front of our very eyes, from the starting point, almost at the top of the mountain, to a 'phenomenon' of sorts by the time the half height had been covered. An alert trekker had seen the first boulder break loose and build up. As luck would have it, we didn't have a video camera handy. We could have filmed a landslide in the early stages of its birth otherwise. The avalanche was headed in the direction we had just covered in the last few minutes and along which about twenty of our fellow-trekkers were headed. There was very little greenery up the mountains, which would arrest the falling boulders and this enabled the group at risk to see the avalanche much before it was down upon them. The trekkers ran back the way they had come and took shelter in a protected area. The SOS for a landslide, in the mountain language, which we were to learn and remember hereafter, is a series of short, sharp and loud whistles which resembles the twitting of birds in its music and catches immediate attention. Once this new knowledge was made known, everyone in our group started practising to whistle in the specified manner, much to the discomfiture of the hill folk.

The Lamari to Budhi stretch passed without further incident and we proceeded only after we had ensured that every person and luggage in the group was accounted for and that the landslide had not accounted for anybody. The distance to Budhi was not much and the ascent wasn't very taxing either. However, the last 1 km or so, was along a sharper incline which made progress slow, and necessitated a 2 - minute halt after every 5 minutes of walking. The approach to Budhi was marked by a bridge over a small rivulet, and just before the bridge, we detected another up-mountain trekking route which bypasses Lamari altogether. We might have missed a dress circle seat on the landslide had we chosen the upper route. However, on our return from Kailash, we were almost forced into the situation of choosing the upper route. Heavy rains had made the path slushy and riskier due to the closeness of the river, and it was with extreme caution and trepidation that we chose the lower trekking route.

Our arrival at the KMVN camp at Budhi was greeted by several hundred brilliantly coloured flowers. The flora at this camp and in its vicinity, are absolutely divine. It is perhaps a unique combination of water, temperature, time and environmental conditions, in an otherwise inhospitable set of circumstances, that brings out the flowers in their fullest bloom. Photographers had a field day, and some of the better photographs on the flowers of the region are shown in Figs. 8-12. At Budhi, we met trekkers from Batch 2 who were returning after their trek to Kailash-Manasarovar. The author (Batch 5) developed a friendship with Mr. Vishwas Gore at Budhi and that association has resulted in this book. Earlier on, between Tawaghat and Pangu, our batch had crossed trekkers from Batch 1. We would meet Batch 3 at Lipulekh Pass, Batch 4 at Taklakot, Batch 6 at Tarchen, Batch 7 at Lipulekh Pass, Batch 8 at Budhi, Batch 9 at Tawaghat and Batch 10 at New Delhi. Clearly, the Kailash-Manasarovar Yatra was planned very well.

Coming back to the Budhi KMVN camp, towards the evening, the trekkers were presented with a cultural show, highlighting the talents of the local Bhotias. The dance and recital show was well received and was authentically Kumaoni. The language is very sweet and is delivered in a sing-song manner. By now, most of us were beginning to appreciate some of the finer nuances, expression tools and figures of speech, quite unique to this mountain dialect. Some of us also penned down the lyrics of the Bhotia songs, verbatim, with assistance from the performers. There is one particular song which comes to memory immediately. It is a description on the Kailash-Manasarovar Yatra from Pangu onwards. Stanzas are repetitive in message and rhyme scheme, and the song is extremely simple hence endearing. Perhaps therein lies its greatest beauty.

**Flora at the Budhi Camp**

Any book on the Kailash-Manasarovar trek via the Lipulekh route must necessarily carry a mention of the exotic floral beauty at Budhi. If there is no such mention, the reader may safely assume that the writer has been constrained to leave such a discussion out. In my opinion, such an omission tantamounts to sacrilege. Not counting fancy flower shows organised at fancier five- star hotels, I may claim in all fairness that nowhere else. have I seen such an impressive array of floral beauties. The flowers were impressive not only for their richness in tone and texture but also for their positioning against each other as well as against a muted background. A few of the best photographs are presented here and it is amazing that the often harsh weather and climatic conditions at a 9,000 feet altitudes can still leave lots of room for rich flora to develop in just a few weeks of sunshine. Dr. Salim Ali's extensive research on the flora of this and nearby regions dates back to 1946 and perhaps the only reason why florists, photographers and botanists haven't really caught on might be the lack of a proper recording, photography and documentation of all things beautiful on this trekking route. The Chrysalis Imperialis variety of the rose, the Himalayan Knotweed, the Himalayan Hogweed, the Himalayan Betony and the Jack in the Pulpit are only a microscopic few of the hundreds of varieties seen and photographed in and around Budhi.

Fig. 8 shows the chrysalis Imperialis variety of the rose and it will be a tragedy if I have to emphasize that this is a rose for in my opinion anything that is said about this photograph will only lessen its impact and beauty. Observe the geometrically shaped petals, their texture, the manner in which they have curled up and the subtle hues and colour variances which mark the inner petals from those along the edges. Some of the petals are seen to fold along sharp faces. I think the beauty of this flower is largely due to its delicately shaped corolla and perhaps also due to the rich colour contrast which the background lends to it.

Another colourful flower has been shown in Fig. 9 and I had to confirm with my Botany schoolteacher that this is indeed the Himalayan Knotweed (*Bistorta affinis* (D. Don) Greene = *Polygonum Affine* D. Don). The herb is densely tufted, forming mats with narrow elliptic leaves and cylindrical spikes of deep pink or even orange flowers borne at the ends of short erect stems. These flowers are common on open slopes, at altitudes of 9,000 feet and above in the months of June to September.

Yet another breath taking beautiful floral representation has been shown in Fig. 10. The Himalayan Hogweed (*Heracleum lanatum* Michx. = *H. candicans Wall.* ex DC) occurs as an erect perennial herb with a stout root-stock, with a hollow pubescent grooved stem, and large pinnate leaves, white on the underside. Flowers are white in many small umbels forming a large umbrella. The herb occurs on open slopes in dry areas in Kashmir and Garhwal in Western and Central Himalayas at altitudes above 6,500 feet. The herb bears flowers in June-July. The roots of this herb are reported to contain a chemical like psoralin which is a photosensitive substance, used in skin therapy.

Another good reason to do botanical research on the Kailash-Manasarovar trail, appears in Fig. 11. The majestic looking flower is the Himalayan Betony (*Stachys sericea Wall.* ex Benth.) is a perennial, erect, silky herb reaching about one metre. It bears a leafy spike of pink flowers in dense whorls and is found from Kashmir to Western Nepal at altitudes above 6,500 feet on meadows and open grass slopes.

The flowers of the region come in a very large variety of forms, fragrances, colours and hues. One delightful species, which resembles a snakehood, has been shown in Fig. 12. The Jack in the Pulpit (*Arisaema propinquum Schott.* = *A. wallichianum Hk.*) is a tuberous herb with 30-60 cms erect aerial stem bearing three leaflets. The flowers are borne on a separate stalk bearing an attractive purple ribbed (striped) hood as of a snake (often, therefore, known as snake lily) tapering to a tail like tip. The stalks of leaf and inflorescence are usually brown spotted. The herb occurs in woodlands and open spaces during May-July, at an altitude above 7,500 feet from Kashmir to Tibet. The tubers (corms) of this genus though rich in starch contain some toxic substances and are at times, used in indigenous medicine. They hibernate during winter and give rise to new plants with the onset of summer rains.

**Budhi to Gunji**

Budhi to Gunji is another very stiff climb, up the Chhia Lekh Pass which forms the high point of the journey. An appropriate synopsis of the trekking route would be a sharp ascent upto Chhia Lekh Pass, up and down upto Garbiang and a flat level table-top for the last 6 km to Gunji. The total distance for the day's trekking is 18 km which takes up about 7 hours.

It was raining incessantly all night and until our departure from Budhi the next morning. The path had become slushy and progress was slow, measured and deliberate in certain sections. Fig. 13 shows trekkers trudging from Budhi to Gunji along a gooey, clayey patch. The men in the picture are just about to go under the spume of a new-born waterfall created by overnight rains in the region. The soil was so well plasticized to the extent that it was impossible for a person to walk single without assistance from someone on firmer terrain. A slip could land someone right into the Kaliganga, several hundred feet below. With safety as the main concern, trekking was carried out in groups of four until the clayey patches were successfully negotiated.

The ascent up the Chhia Lekh Pass is very difficult and edges along the Kaliganga river almost at the water level. It has been attempted to demonstrate the power of this river using a few photographs. Surprisingly, in almost 200 photographs that the author has seen or taken on the river, the Kaliganga seems to possess a knack for looking very tame and docile and the 'washing machine' effect seen so dominatingly in real life, does not transfer well on film. A few faithful reproductions have been included in this section and must be used as an indicator that the river's presence is not to be taken lightly. A river crossing without using the bridge, is absolutely out of the question. As seen in Fig. 14, the Kaliganga river is most intimidating in the Budhi to Gunji stretch for the one reason that the trekking path is at the water level. The river behaves like one in chaos and personally, I have never known a large-scaled turbulence to be so multi-directional, as this and the next photograph indicate. The river can sweep you off your feet in more ways than one. One doesn't know what word to use in the description of this river: arrogance or majesty.

Another view is shown in Fig. 15 and to be a little honest with the readers, after this photograph was printed, I had a little trouble identifying which side is up. Nevertheless, turbulence is turbulence even if it is upside-down. The river emerges from the top left corner, thrashes about wildly towards the right and the centre of the photograph and neatly collects in a cavern at the bottom middle and flows away along the bottom right corner. Note the signs of erosive wear on the rock midstream. Any guesses how long before the rock is dislodged and washed away? What a pity this ain't milkshake or whipped cream. If washing machines get to be this efficient, they'd throw the washerwoman out of business. As regards adventure sports, I'd like to see the Old Spice Aftershave fellow perform his fancy stunts here. The Physics schoolmaster from West Bengal calls it "the river gone crazy". Our group also had a champion swimmer who had covered most of the major straits in the world and all he could say at this spot was: "Thank God! I am on vacation".

The Chhia Lekh Pass ascent took up almost two and a half hours of determined trekking after which the trail to Garbiang was a gentle up and down, upstream of the Kaliganga. Budhi to Garbiang is a 10 km walk which took up about 4 hours. Trekkers stopped at Garbiang for a while to drink mountain tea while their companions who were left behind caught up with them.

Garbiang is a unique village. It lies on the right bank of the Kaliganga at an elevation of 1000 feet above the water level. The village is gradually sinking into the river since it is not based upon solid rock, but on loose, porous soil which is continually eroded by the river. The sinking village was visited by a few Prime Ministers of India and several geological survey teams have recommended that nothing could be done to prevent the village from sinking and that it must be abandoned. Very few people live in Garbiang today, most have left for more secure holdings. The village has a Post Office and a few two and three storeys buildings with an impressive artistry on the doorways; but the message is loud and clear: Occupations and households have long since moved out of Garbiang. Incidentally, everyone from Garbiang has one common surname: Garbyal. Just like the Budhiyals from Budhi, the Napalchials from Napalchu and the Gunjials from Gunji.

The trekking route to Gunji passes through Garbiang and proceeds along an absolutely flat table-top route for a major portion of the journey. Occasional ascents and descents break the monotony in an otherwise level piece of trekking. The KMVN camp at Gunji can be seen from about 5 km away and gives the impression of being very close; but there is a huge circuitous route upstream of the Kaliganga and later, upstream of the Kuti until the town of Napalchu, crossing the Kuti and retracing the downstream path upto the Kuti-Kaliganga confluence, almost in a full-circle route. The destination is always within sight and the irony is that it takes almost three hours to reach Gunji after its first sighting.

Fig. 16 shows a frontal view of the KMVN camp at Gunji. For the first time on the trek the 10,000 foot altitude barrier has been crossed. Gunji has a Post Office and perhaps the last Bank before the International Border. Gunji also has an ITBP hospital where yatris are checked for high altitude illness symptoms. The Kaliganga river emerges from the left-centre of the photograph and flows along the valley between the two sloping mountain ranges (into the plane of this book). The Kuti river which arrives from Zollingkong in the vicinity of Mount Adi Kailash emerges from the bottom right corner of the photograph and meets the Kaliganga in the vicinity of the Gunji camp. The greenery of the terrain decreases sharply here onwards and the barren bald face of the mountain on the right is devoid of vegetation possibly due to a combination of factors such as altitude and more importantly from high velocity cold winds which whirlpool through the valley. Lastly, and I hope the photographic resolution transfers well during publishing, the flat piece of land seen in the bottom centre, located behind all the huts, on the other side of the Kuti is the plateau over which the Budhi-Gunji trekking path lies. Believe it or not, the plateau in question is at least five kilometres away. The trekkers need to take a long circuit before a crossing over the *Kuti* can be made.Trekking progress is slow because Gunji lies at a high altitude of 10,625 feet and after having walked the last 15 km at altitudes above 9,000 feet, the first signs of strain begin to show up. However, the trekkers will rapidly get used to small increases in altitudes and high altitude physiological and emotional changes will stabilise over a period of time. Nevertheless, in view of the less amount of oxygen, even simple tasks such as tying up of shoelaces can be very tiring and every activity is laborious and is done only if considered absolutely essential.

**On Gunji**

Gunji has the last Post Office in India along the Lipulekh-Gurla Mandhata corridor. It also has a bank which remains open in the six summer months of the year, upto October 31st. In winters, the terrain is covered with snow and everyone moves down to Dharchula. The trekkers began to wonder when the bankmen did their yearly auditing and what date they called their "year ending". The bank has only one employee who has been saddled with many responsibilities and to us, the bank looked more an exercise in fun than in utility.

Gunji also has an ITBP camp and some basic medical facilities. All the yatris were examined here for blood pressure and general fitness, especially those who were a borderline pass at the ITBP Hospital in Delhi. Everyone seemed to be okay and chose to spend the evening exploring the town. The locals seemed pleased to take us around and practically everywhere we saw delicate interwoven artistry on the door panels and other items of woodwork. We were also taken to the village square where a story on the heroism, truthfulness and strength of a Kumaoni woman was told to us by proud descendants who have built a rock monument in the lady warrior's memory.

It was late in the evening when we returned from the village. It was drizzling lightly and winds would get colder as the night progressed. We all had a quick dinner and decided to call it a day. The long day's trek and the evening's outing had left us considerably drained. 'Tomorrow onwards we start trekking in the high altitudes' was one thought that occupied every mind. Nobody was scared, they were all charged with excitement. The next day was eagerly awaited.

A sketch of the trekking distances in India, from the starting point at Tawaghat to the end point at Lipulekh Pass, as also the absolute distance from New Delhi, along with ascents and descents for each segment and altitudes of each camp, in feet and metres, is presented in Fig. 17.

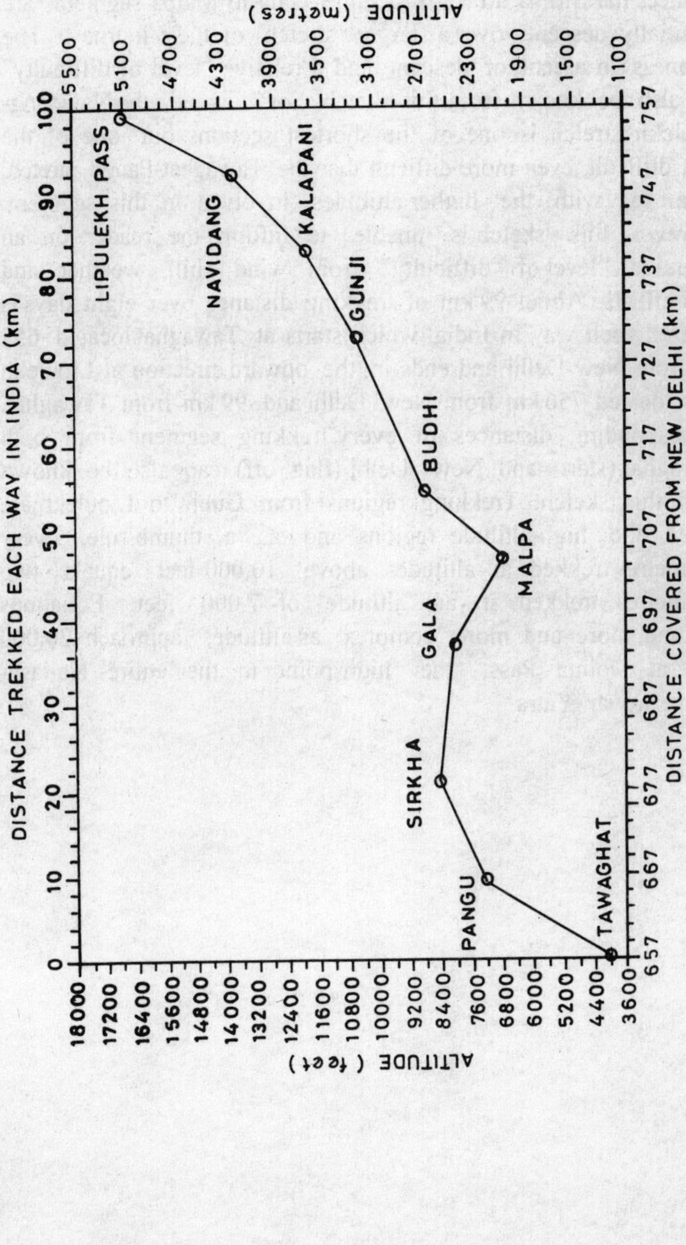


*Fig. 17.* A Destination-Distance-Altitude-Inclination map of the Indian section of the Kailash-Manasarovar Yatra.

This figure is a sketch of the Trekking Distances in India versus their altitude (both in feet and metres). On the Indian section of the journey, not all segments involve ascents. For instance, the Sirkha to Gala and the Gala to Malpa segments are essentially descents over a larger stretch of their journey. The steepness in ascent or descent, and a relative "level of difficulty" can also be known from this sketch. For example, the Navidang-Lipulekh stretch is one of the shortest sections, but one of the most difficult, even more difficult than the Tawaghat-Pangu stretch, more so, with the higher altitudes involved in this segment. However, this sketch is unable to inform the reader on an increased "level of difficulty" from wind chill, weather and river effects. About 99 km of trekking distance over eight days is covered each way in India, which starts at Tawaghat located 657 km from New Delhi and ends in the onward direction at Lipulekh Pass located 756 km from New Delhi and 99 km from Tawaghat. Corresponding distances of every trekking segment from both Tawaghat (start) and New Delhi (flag off) can also be known from this sketch. Trekking regions from Gunji to Lipulekh are called the high-altitude regions and as a thumb rule, every kilometre trekked at altitudes above 10,000 feet equals two kilometres trekked at an altitude of 7,000 feet. Equations become more and more complex as altitudes approach 20,000 feet at Dolma Pass, the high point in the entire Kailash-Manasarovar Yatra.

*Fig. 18.*

19 8 '96

*Fig. 20.*

*Fig. 21.*

*Fig. 22.*

28 8 '96

*Fig. 24.*

*Fig. 25*

3

# Trekking in the High Altitudes (Gunji and Beyond)

The region from Gunji to Lipulekh Pass can be called the high-altitude region. The International border is about 26 km away from Gunji and all locations in this route are at altitudes above 10,625 feet. Trees grow more and more scarce and after a while, landscapes appear barren and mountainscapes totally bald and devoid not only of vegetation but also of beauty. Occasionally, snow-capped mountain peaks may be seen in the distance. Trekking routes become very broad, at least 8 feet in width, and the river does not appear as intimidating as it did at lower altitudes. At the higher altitudes, many trekkers complain of a drowsiness towards the early mornings and a general drowsiness which persists all throughout the day. Trekkers prefer to walk slowly and reduce their trekking pace to about 2 km per hour.

From Gunji to Navidang and back again on the return journey, the trekkers remain under the care and vigil of the jawans of the Indo-Tibetan Border Police. Trekkers must stay close to each other and in view of its strategic significance, loitering is prohibited. The ITBP jawans are perhaps the best mountain-trekking specimens one can come across and they prove to be an inspiration to many an advanced trekker. In instances where trekking deadlines have to be met, such as the Lipulekh Pass crossing, the ITBP jawans ensure that everybody reaches the border at the prescribed hour; and they will drive the trekkers real hard if they have to, in order to ensure a timely border crossing and handing over to the Tibetan authorities.

## Gunji to Kalapani

The Gunji to Kalapani route takes the trekker from an altitude of 10,625 feet to 11,880 feet, over a distance of 10 km. The trekking time is about 5 hours, inclusive of a 15-minute break in which the ITBP escorts make arrangements to serve tea.

The Gunji to Kalapani segment is extremely picturesque. Trekking paths are extremely wide, to the extent of being called motorable, in many sections. The Kaliganga river does not pose a threat to life or limb, it flows quietly, at a safe distance away. Nepal lies on the opposite bank, and an occasional Nepali house may be seen on the far side. Fig. 18 shows a photograph of a Nepali house taken from the Indian side, over the Kaliganga river. Several mountain ranges, one behind the other may be seen in the background. The trees are probably deciduous in character and are used as firewood and in construction. I think the house looks very quaint and anyone interested in acquiring property here is advised to prospect left wards while trekking from Gunji to Kalapani. The house is located approximately midway. However, don't ask me what the householder does for a living, I don't know!

At a few places, the trekking path takes a few steep up or down gradients, but overall, the route is along a flat-land. The trekkers get the impression of walking along a meadow. However, landslides are quite common and the trekkers are advised to occasionally glance upwards at the mountains. There are no villages or settlements beyond Gunji and the familiar sight of runny-nosed kids, in embarrassingly ripped off trousers, chanting *Om Namah Shivaya* and expecting some money or food from each yatri is not available any more. On the return journey, these children might find the yatris to be more generous and polite. It is surprising what Kailash can do to you!

Just before the approach to Kalapani, the source of the Kaliganga river, the trekkers can see a towering cliff to the left. These are the Vyas mountains and located almost at their top, is the Vyas Cave, where the accomplished sage is said to had done an extensive penance. The mountains are denuded of their greenery and colour shades, and look extremely ferocious and intimidating. The Vyas Cave is said to be of the size of a huge conference hall and the only approach is from the top.

Fig. 19 shows a photograph of the Vyas mountains taken from the KMVN-ITBP camp at Kalapani. The horizontal distance from the point of photography to the foot of the mountains is about 2 km and the height of the uppermost peak (partly masked by clouds) is at least 2,000 feet above the point of photography (which itself is at about 11,880 feet). The tree-line altitude has been crossed and sources of vegetation and greenery are scarce. The mountain appears barren and extremely wind eroded. An opening into the mountains may be seen towards the centre of the photograph. This is the Vyas Cave where the great saint is said to have done penance several centuries ago. I wonder if Tom Sawyer knew of this hideout. The cave however is very big and has a diameter of about 50 feet at its mouth. Locals insist that it is as big as a huge conference hall and can accommodate upto a thousand people (who in the world would want to hold conference there?). For adventure seekers however, there is good news. A brave woman got into the cave a few years back. It was difficult to climb straight up so she took another route which led her to the peak from where she dropped down using a rope, to gain entry into the cave. Any takers for this year?

The Kaliganga river originates from the Shiva-Parvati and Vaishnodevi temple at Kalapani. This is the first time that trekkers actually go to the left bank of the river, after an academic foray into Nepal at Dharchula. The temple at Kalapani is run and maintained by the ITBP. It is obvious that the temple is run with a missionary zeal by the jawans who do their religious service more out of a pleasure than as an obligation. *Jai Mata Di* has been inscribed in large letters, high into the mountains above the temple. Fig. 20 shows a view of the Shiva-Parvati and Vaishnodevi temple at Kalapani. The Kaliganga river originates as a small brook in the rocks behind this temple, collects to form a pool shown in the foreground and cascades to form the turbulent river. The Kaliganga separates India from Nepal and the land at the source of the river was procured from the Nepal Government in exchange for another piece near Dharchula. This is the only occasion, after Dharchula that the trekkers could go onto the left river bank. The temple is maintained well by the ITBP in spite of the fact that the area is inhabited only in the summer months. All items of religious worship and decorations have been very innovatively, tastefully and painstakingly acquired. There is no electricity in these parts so audio taped and recorded bhajans, singing the praise of Lord Shiva, are played over a music system which runs on a 12V battery which perhaps, rightfully belongs under the bonnet of a military truck.

In the winters, the area is under a snow cover. All activity then shifts its centre of operation to Dharchula. The camp is closed in the cold months of the year.

All yatris must deposit their passports at the small Customs Checkpost at Kalapani. These are stamped, dated and endorsed for authentic transport into Tibet through the Lipulekh Pass. The Ponymen and porters also submit their service passes which are returned to them on their way back. Additionally, all, or at least a major portion of the Indian currency with each yatri must be deposited with the ITBP personnel. Carriage of large amounts of money through the border where it may influence lifestyles, opinions or loyalties is not permitted. The money is returned to the yatris at Kalapaṇi, when they return from Kailash-Manasarovar.

**Kalapani to Navidang**

The Kalapani to Navidang stretch is quite easy in pace and climb. Trekkers ascend from 11,880 feet to 13,800 feet over a distance of 9 km. The trekking time, inclusive of a 15-minute tea break, is about 5 hours. Yatris leave Kalapani at about 6.00 a.m. and arrive at Navidang by 11.00 a.m.

In the 9 km stretch, trekkers can observe the terrain acquire a new wardrobe. The greenery from the mountains is stripped and replaced with a stark, jagged mountain nakedness. Two photographs taken between Kalapani and Navidang demonstrate the two extremes in vegetation. Fig. 21 shows an unusual tree formation along the Kalapani-Navidang route. This is in fact a two-tree system in which both trees have grown identically, yet independently to produce a marvel in symmetry. I think this photograph is eloquent in many respects other than the one just stated. For instance, the tree-line for this mountain series is clearly marked, traversing the mountain range towards the centre of the photograph. Regions below this line are rich in greenery, and those above are absolutely barren. A thick cloud cover near some of the taller peaks in the region may be noticed. A glacial mountain stream which ultimately meets the Kaliganga, can be seen in the valley. The loose rocks scattered all over the terrain are the result of landslides over weak, labile mountains.

Fig. 22 is an object-oriented photograph (as against a laity-oriented photograph which is used to document marriages or other events) in which the central theme is to show extremely barren, jagged mountains seen during the trek from Kalapani to Navidang. Climbing becomes increasingly difficult at higher altitudes. As air gets rarer, breathing becomes increasingly laborious. Short 10-15 minute breaks become necessary after an hour's trekking. At one such break, the ITBP make tea and light snacks available. The breaks are typically used to adjust camera settings, to exchange trekking ideas or sometimes only to regain breath. Observe the landslide boulders strewn across the terrain as also the snowy deposits in some parts of the precipitous mountains. The surroundings are observed to be extremely barren. Here onwards, until return to Kalapani, tree sightings will be very uncommon. High altitude regions such as these, in which there is plenty of water, but no plant life, are classified as "cold deserts".

The KMVN camp at Navidang is situated at a very scenic location. From the camp, the trekkers can see several mountain ranges harmoniously blending into each other in the neighbourhood of Navidang. The first, and perhaps a sight which cannot be ignored on a clear day, shown in Fig. 24 is that of the Om Parvat. High up into the mountains, at least a few thousand feet above the KMVN camp at Navidang (13,800 feet) and staring out at the observer is a large inscription of the 'Om', inscribed in Devanagari, on the rock surface and further embossed with pearly white snow which imparts an aura to the divine calligraphy. The lettering of the Om is complete with the 'Chandrabindu' and radiates a spatial emanence. As to how the inscription of the Om was created, an entire religious treatise can be written. Possibly, inscription is an improper word to use in this context: divine chiselling might be more accurate.

An interaction with previous Kailash-Manasarovar yatris and a discussion on their archival photographs, reveals that the font and the shape of the Om lettering change every season, possibly due to changing mountain dynamics and forces. The "divine handwriting" seems to get better with the passage of time. It is amazing, however, that the mountain push-pull forces have never distorted the calligraphy (including the Chandrabindu). In the photograph of the Om Parvat, the barren rock to snow to deep blue sky contrast is striking. The terrain and the clouds do not distract the viewer from the central theme of the photograph, rather, they beautifully complement the land-mountain-sky interface.

One photograph which precedes the Om Parvat is that of the cloud-covered Om Parvat. In this photograph, shown in figure 23, to dramatise the before and after effect, the landscape is that of a cold desert. The river bed is extremely slushy and the mountain soil is very loose. The weather in places such as these changes without notice or warning. Within a few minutes, the field of view may become blistering hot, or may worsen to a blizzard. Perhaps, it was a set of circumstances such as these which caused a tourist helicopter to crash into the mountains a few years back. The grateful survivors have today, built a temple at the site. A medical emergency here is the last thing anyone would want. The nearest medical aid is a seven-day walk away.

When our trekking group arrived at Navidang, the Om Parvat was under a cloud cover. We waited all day for the clouds to lift. The inscription, about which I had heard a lot, remained hidden for the entire day. The trek to and over the Lipulekh Pass was to begin early the next morning at about 4.00 a.m. and it was quite certain that the Om would not make itself visible before we left. Everyone in the trek hoped for better luck on our return. We were singularly lucky in this regard. On the return stretch, the Om was all aglow and remained so for the next several hours. The photograph used in this book shows the Om Parvat in its full celestial costume.

After an early and light dinner, the trekkers chose to close shop by about 8.30 p.m. The next day's trek to and beyond the Lipulekh Pass was thought to be the hardest and most dangerous segment of the trek. Inclines were close to being perpendicular in a few instances and snow had to be trudged through towards the final stages of the journey. As these thoughts passed through each mind, faces acquired grim, resolute expressions. Everyone was charging himself up, motivating himself and egging himself on. We could hear a blizzard howling and screeching in the valley, over and about the curved tin roofs of our lodgings and we began to wonder if the Bernoulli principles on turbulence in fluid media were valid at high altitudes. Trekkers were asked to refrain from opening either of the doors located at opposite faces of a missile shaped residential dome. The residential quarters were aerodynamically shaped and in the face of the tempest outside, everyone prepared themselves for a guided aerial tour over the Om Parvat in the middle of the night.

The next morning, there was good news and bad news. The good news was that we had survived the storm. The bad news was, it was raining heavily.

**Navidang to Lipulekh Pass**

Bad news travels faster than good news, sometimes even without a communication medium. If you don't believe it, I would like to point out that it took only a few seconds for the nearly 30 trekkers, 28 porters, 35 ponies, 15 ponymen and about 15 ITBP jawans to realise that it was raining heavily outside and that the Lipulekh ascent had suddenly increased in difficulty by a factor of ten. The 4:00 a. m. departure was rescheduled to 4:30 a.m. by the ITBP personnel, hoping that the rains would stop by then. Well, they did certainly reduce in intensity and brought down the Difficulty Factor to about a third of its maximum value.

A point that needs mention here, is that all cameras, including camcorders, must necessarily be emptied before a cross-over into Tibet. A new roll or tape must be loaded and that too, only after crossing over into Tibet. Yatris must plan their photography so that they have only a few exposures remaining by the time they reach Navidang. The ITBP personnel do not permit transport of exposed photographic films into Tibet, and their concern for National Interest and safety is fully justified. Photographs of the terrain and of the Lipulekh Pass may be taken on the return journey without reserve. The ITBP is quite firm and insists on opening up the cameras even if the film is only a few exposures old. I would advise the yatris to plan their photography from Gunji onwards and avoid unnecessary arguments and negotiations with the Border Police. Rolls and tapes are marked and returned to the yatris on their return to India.

Finally, at 4.30 a.m, the ITBP personnel thought it was time to move on. The caravan started for Lipulekh in one single file. The 7 km trek to Lipulekh Pass was to take the trekkers from an altitude of 13,800 feet to an altitude of 16,730 feet. Under ideal conditions, the trek takes about 3 hours, though the ITBP personnel cover the distance within one and a half hours in an emergency. The scheduled time for our batch to reach Lipulekh Pass was no later than 8.00 a.m. IST (or 10.30 a.m. Chinese time). Batch 3 would cross over into India from Tibet and our batch (Batch 5) would cross over into Tibet. On crossing over the international border guides, ponies, porters and escorts would be exchanged between batches. The ITBP authorities would hand over the yatris from Batch 5 to the Chinese representative and take over Batch 3 from him. The yatris coming into India enjoy the right of way, along the Lipulekh Pass. The Chinese representatives do not wait for the incoming batch if it does not arrive at the scheduled hour. They hand over the batch and leave if they do not find the next one in preparedness. It is essential that batches going into Tibet reach at least 30 minutes before 8.00 a.m. In any case, yatris can descend into Tibet only after the earlier batch has arrived and everybody and every item has been accounted for.

In an effort to ensure that our batch reached Lipulekh on time, the ITBP jawans egged us on relentlessly, more so because we had started late. No resting time was allowed. People were gasping for breath. Trekkers above the age of 40, and whoever found the fast-paced walking difficult, were forcibly put upon horses. A continuous drizzle which was to last for the next few hours, a dense misty fog, newborn mountain streams frequently crossing the trekking route, difficulty in breathing, a biting cold, a fierce wind, poor visibility, especially because dawn had yet to crack, all combined to produce an effect which had even toughened trekkers crying. A few senior people had to be administered with oxygen before their speech regained coherence. Some trekkers had become cranky and started arguing with the Border Police who bore everything with a 'We've seen it all before' expression. The trek to Lipulekh seemed to last forever. Our escorts kept vigil on everyone and did not let anybody lag. When horses were seen to be in short supply and trekking spirits almost broken, a few disoriented trekkers were bodily lifted and carried by the Border Police on their shoulders. I like to think of myself as an advanced trekker, but on watching the ITBP go about their tasks with an 'all in a day's work' attitude, I was learning a new lesson in mountain trekking. In case, I happen to write a book on the ITBP sometime, I plan to give it the title: 'Iron Fist in a Velvet Glove'.

Everybody was brought to the Indian side of the Lipulekh Pass, a good half hour before the scheduled time.

Fig. 25 shows the Lipulekh Pass which is the high point (16,730 feet) of the trekking on the Indian side. From a security standpoint, photography is prohibited while entering Tibet through this route, though photographs may be taken on the return journey. This photograph too was taken on the return journey and is used at this point only for illustrative purposes. The Great Tibetan Plateau is at an altitude of about 15,000 feet (spread over several hundred kilometres of terrain) and a descent from the Lipulekh Pass is very sharp. Seen here, is a group of yatris returning to India from Tibet and photographed at the halfway point at about 7.00 a.m. IST. The ascent has actually begun from several hundred feet below, where a few people can be spotted.

Trekking is done over a sheet of snow. This bit of trekking is the one awaited with most trepidation. Visibility can be reduced to a few feet at times, there is no established trekking path, there is no indication as to which bit of snow is firm and which is not, storms and gales which may lift people and equipment like leaves, are not uncommon, landslides may occur, the snow may start melting when the sun comes strong and even otherwise, it is beastly cold, to say the least. To use a euphemism, a few people haven't been quite lucky here. As a precaution, this section must be trekked before 7.30 a.m. Indian time (10.00 a.m. in China) and in an effort to ensure that this schedule is met with, the ITBP personnel drive and prod the trekkers on incessantly until they have finally crossed over. Senior trekkers may require an oxygen supplement which is invariably carried by all groups. Lipulekh is the third crossing point in the Kailash-Manasarovar Yatra. When the third batch returns to India, the fifth batch crosses over into Tibet. Escorts, guides, porters and ponies hand over one batch of yatris and take in another.

Fig. 26 shows another view of the Lipulekh Pass incline. The climb over the Lipulekh glacier which finally leads to India on the return journey starts here. The trekking path starts from bottom-left and proceeds up the mountain on the right. Progress is excruciatingly slow and it takes over an hour to cover the approximately 500 metre distance to the Indian border. Auli, Narkanda and several alpine slopes not withstanding, the descent might make an excellent skiing circuit were it not for defence considerations.

**On Lipulekh Pass**

Spending time at the Lipulekh Pass, waiting for the earlier batch to arrive before trekkers may descend into Tibet, is not exactly, a very pleasurable activity, but it is thrilling nevertheless. Standing at the Indian edge of the pass, is like standing at the brink of a precipice, or rather, at the very edge of an immensely steep skiing slope. The first rays of the sun filtering through the clouds at about 8.00 a.m. present a fairly scary picture. You are positioned at a point of great height. There is hardly any reference point at the same level as you, other than snow laden mountains in every direction excepting in the front, which is where you have to go. Every other point is several thousand feet below. The downward slope into Tibet can be seen only if you crane your neck forward and in any case, though one has to travel only about 400 metres before ponies from the previous batch are available, the pony point cannot be seen from the top of the pass. Strong winds and gales which threaten to sweep you into Tibet howl incessantly through the valley. When the sun gathers in intensity, the snow on the mountain sides begins to melt, making trekking a very dangerous form of indulgence. With this factor in mind, the cross-over time has been decided as 8.00 a.m. IST or 10.30 a.m. Chinese time. The strong and cold winds make it necessary to seek shelter in leeward rocky shelter a little before the pass. Swami Pranavananda says that on a clear day, the Kailash and the Gurla Mandhata can be seen from the Lipulekh Pass in a direct line of sight. I could not verify this claim, visibility was low while going to Tibet and again while returning to India, thirteen days later.

**Waiting at Lipulekh**

After what seemed like hours, the first lot of trekkers from Batch 3 could be seen trudging up the Lipulekh Pass from the Tibetan side. Some of my batchmates were growing to be a little miserable by this time and had to be shown that the earlier batch was arriving before their spirits started reviving. It took about 20 minutes more for the entire batch to reach the top and another 20 minutes for the luggage to arrive while administrative formalities were attended to. This gave us some time to interact with the earlier batch, exchange addresses and request messages to be relayed wherever possible. Finally, when all the procedures were attended to, the ITBP wished us good luck and left for Navidang with the batch that had just arrived while we descended into Tibet along the "ski route", very gingerly at first and even more gingerly later on as we saw trekkers slipping very frequently and bruising themselves in the process. The descent to the pony point took about an hour. Of course, photography was not allowed while crossing the pass, but to illustrate the set of conditions that exist at the pass, a few representative photographs taken on the return journey, have been introduced into this section.

Yatris from the previous batch appeared to have been savagely sun burnt and considerably thinned down. They all looked like lean, mean trekkers and appeared very happy and rather relieved to return to India.

**Towards Taklakot**

Well ultimately, we did reach the pony point from where we were transported on horseback to a bus which was waiting for us a few kilometres away. It took a little more than an hour to reach the bus, which was located across a stream which the horses waded across. Everybody clambered onto the bus. There was another truck nearby which was to bring our luggage. The next halt was to be the Pulan Guest House at Taklakot, about 15 km away along a terrain of rubble and stones. The journey would take over an hour. We had finally arrived in Tibet and for the first time since we awoke at Navidang early in the morning, we found time to exchange pleasantries and look at the Tibetan skies through the wide panel windows in the bus.

We advanced our watches to the Tibetan time and remarked that the Tibetan horses were indeed of a sturdy build and a regal bearing. A typical horse back was at least six feet above the ground which necessitated some acrobatics with three and four layers of insulating clothing. Ladies and senior men had to be hauled so that they could ride comfortably. Well come to think of it, a small ladder does form an integral part of every mountain trekking kit and might have proved handy if we had cared to carry the full kit.

We were to discover later that there are two races in Tibet, each with distinct physical features and differences. The athletic, 6 foot tall warrior race with long faces, lean build, Russian facial features and a rough manner was a species seen in the Kailash Khanda (Tarchen). These people drove yaks through the Kailash parikrama and fed on yak produce. The other race was a delicately built, slim, short species of a little more refinement and possessed chiselled Mongolian facial features and gave the impression of being a little more educated and exposed to the winds of change. They worked as ponymen during the Manasarovar parikrama and were seen in the Manas Khanda and sometimes tilled the land. Before the reader begins to draw parallels from H. G. Well's Time Machine let me dispel all notions on Morlocks or Elois: both the Tibetan races are extremely hardworking, the horsemen a little more friendly, but both essentially untouched and unchanged through centuries. More in amusement than out of malice, both rubbed their hands in glee whenever someone fell off his horse or yak. Neither of them spoke or understood English or Hindi and spoke only Tibetan which was beyond our comprehension. Communication was through gestures but it was not difficult to judge that the rustic Tibetans looked upon us as quaint artefacts in the same manner that we regarded them. Over the next few days, we were to closely observe each other's way of life and learn from each other. Swami Pranavananda has discussed the Tibetan way of life in great depth in his book, in the chapter on Human Geography and has very elegantly evaluated the influences from the Kazakh nomads from Russia on Tibetan tribal dwellings. Swami Pranavananda's book forms one of the greatest inspirations for this adventure documentation.

# 4

# On the Tibetan Plateau

## Getting Used to Different Time Zones

Geographically, Taklakot lies at the latitude of Chandigarh and at the longitude of Allahabad and the town is only 20 km away from the Lipulekh post at the Indian border. However, given the "width" of China (of which Tibet Autonomous forms a part) and the legendary Chinese fondness to follow "one single time" based on Beijing's location which is on the same longitude as Perth (Western Australia) leads to a most unusual situation, chronometry-wise. Sunrise occurs at 8.30 a.m. and sunset at 10.00 p.m. (2.30 hours lead over India).

For any devout Indian who performs *prahar* or time-dependent religious ceremonies, the 6.00 a.m. and sunrise synchronicity is lost. As a result, the Indian religious calendar needs to be adjusted to an extent and there is a sufficient amount of flexibility in the timing of any religious ritual. Marriages may be solemnised and performed at any hour of the day. The morning meal (the equivalent of breakfast) is taken a little before noon and the afternoon repast timed at about 4.00 p.m. Dinners are taken at about 8.00 p.m. and it strikes me as an oddity that three meals occur in a space of eight hours during the day, whilst there is no formal eating activity scheduled in the remaining sixteen!

The Tibetan time and way of life take a little getting used to. Even the food for that matter, most of which is quite similar to what you get in wayside Chinese food-stalls in Mumbai. The question is, would you like to eat it thrice a day for fifteen successive days. In my opinion, you need to have a taste for Chinese (and Tibetan) food. Either you like the food a lot, or you don't in which case you very nearly starve. I must say, in Taklakot, I had a jolly good time, gastronomically speaking. I used to look forward to meal-times. Petite Tibetan women used to sound the gong signifying that the tables were laid and people who came in late were turned away.

On arrival at the Pulan Guest House at Taklakot, we were assigned well furnished quarters with four persons to a room. The dwellings were quite luxurious. In order to complete the immigration formalities, we were required to fill in a form specifying camera make and other trivial details. The payment of $ 500 for further arrangements to Kailash and Manasarovar was made. The next day, we were taken to the bank for foreign exchange which was dealt out in crisp, new currency notes. The banking staff was courteous and very efficient, quite unlike that expected in remote towns and villages. Fig. 27 is a photograph of a Chinese Bank in Taklakot where a US Dollar to Yuan conversion is arranged. Quite a fancy bank for a mofussil location, I must say. It reminds me of the Holiday Inn Crowne Plaza in Delhi. Roads all over Tibet are fairly wide and I suppose it does not take much to build roads on a table-top plateau, at least in the larger towns. Vehicles travel American style as regards side preference and location of steering. I found a Toyota Land Cruiser to be a vehicle better suited to changes in terrain as compared to a Mitsubishi Pajero. Trees in Tibet are a rarity and the bank has two of them. Possibly, these are money plants! The noticeboard outside the bank, written in Chinese, probably carries the name of the bank for this surely couldn't read "No Entry". Observe the dainty mosaic work on the compound walls and a small shop at the left of the photograph.

### What to See and What to Buy in Taklakot

The Taklakot market is about 4 km from the Pulan Guest House and generally, the tourist guide makes arrangements for the entire group to be transported to the marketplace. However, I would recommend walking to the market place and inspecting the numerous sandstone deposits on the way and watching the Chinese army grow potatoes in wayside farms. You don't cross many people returning from the market, but the occasional sight of a mischievous brat being unceremoniously slung over his pygmied, yet muscular father's shoulders can be quite entertaining. I preferred to walk rather than take the bus.

I noticed a peculiar thing about the Taklakot market and shops. Nobody knew how much to charge you. There was no concept of a fixed price even in government controlled shops. Consequently, every commodity was priced on the shopkeeper's perception of your ability to pay, your need for the merchandise being handled and your bargaining ability.

I picked up a good pair of yak-skin trekking shoes and I thought they were the most comfortable pair of shoes I had ever worn. When I asked the shopkeeper how much they would cost (he spoke only Tibetan which I couldn't understand so we talked by punching digits on a calculator to signify expected prices) he, very cautiously punched in 100 signifying 100 Yuan (approximately Rs. 425) looking at me all the while. "Nonsense" I replied, punching in 30 and trying to look absolutely shocked. Within a few minutes, the sale was closed at 40 Yuan. I read somewhere that this is the way the Russians negotiate. I must say the strategy worked fairly well.

The other chaps in the group got wind of this transaction and hounded me to deal on their behalf. Well would you believe it, in a short while, I was negotiating for a hundred pairs of shoes. Everybody had somebody who would be interested in something unique from Tibet. Fourth cousins once removed and distant relatives from Timbuktu were suddenly remembered.

But personal digs apart, there is a lot that the Tibetan market at Taklakot has to offer in terms of quality and lasting value. Large, brilliantly coloured 2 litre thermos flasks, capable of retaining water at 90° C for over eight hours may be had for about 50 Yuan and may be a good purchase. Jewellery, precious stones and necklaces may be obtained at 10-200 Yuan. Woollens, large overalls, Chinese style multipurpose trousers and small locks might be worthwhile acquisitions. Crystal wine glasses, daintily coloured and delicately shaped soup bowls and crockery would perhaps be a novelty. I would recommend buying an abacus. It is authentically Chinese and looks neat on your mantelpiece. A large one costs 20 Yuan. Music fans might find Tibetan music quite upbeat, it is more westernised than Oriental. Some audio cassettes might help in evocative reconstruction. I would also recommend a purchase of Tibetan daggers. I have seen the Tibetans use a dagger as a multipurpose tool and even as a can-opener. Nothing is grown in Tibet, not at least on a large scale and much of the foodstuff and even drink arrives from up-country in cans. The small palm-sized dagger (with its attendant scabbard) would cost 15 Yuan and a long one which resembles King Arthur's Excalibur, complete with a yak-bone grip, would set you back by about 85 Yuan. No, you don't run into problems with the Chinese Customs provided you place the knives into your luggage which the Chinese porter will carry.

It has been about a year since I went to Kailash. The trekking shoes I purchased in Taklakot are still in extensive use and have a lot of life left in them. As regards my abacus, well I haven't learnt to use it still. Anyone who doesn't believe the abacus can work fast is advised to read 'Surely you're Joking Mr. Feynman' in which a wily Oriental with his abacus almost got the better of a Nobel Prize winning scientist in the simple science of calculation.

Ah yes, Taklakot also has a discotheque. But whether you should go there or not is upto you, you are supposed to be on pilgrimage. At least officially, that is.

**A Bit of Indian Heritage in Taklakot**

India has had a trade relationship with Tibet for several hundred years and for a while, parts of Tibet were under Indian rule, notably in the time of the Great Gurus. General Zorawar Singh, the Commander-in-Chief of Maharaja Gulab Singh's army reached Kailash via Jammu and Ladakh in 1841, not as a pilgrim but as a brave conqueror. To use Swami Pranavananda's expression, he pillaged all the villages and gompas and destroyed every fort on his way and expanded the boundaries of the Great Punjab to include all of the present day Pakistan, some parts of Afghanistan, present day Punjab, Haryana, Himachal Pradesh, Kashmir, Ladakh and portions of Tibet. If you look at the Oxford School Atlas you will discover to your amazement that this expanse is about half the size of present day India.

With Tirthapuri (near Taklakot) as his headquarters and with only 1500 men at his command, Zorawar Singh fought a bloody battle at Parkha (midway between Tarchen and Horche) against about 10,000 Tibetans (of the Hun dynasty) and routed them and advanced to Taklakot. The General left his army at Taklakot under the command of his deputy Captain Basti Ram and left for Gartok to attend to some domestic matters. On his return, near Toyo, about 3 km from Taklakot, he was attacked by a big Chinese army sent to assist the Tibetans. Hopelessly outnumbered he battled valiantly for over three hours, to the extent that the Tibetans thought him to be a *tantrik* endowed with supernatural powers. Since it was commonly perceived that no lead or common-metal bullet could penetrate his body, he was killed by a specially designed gold bullet. Only in order to ensure that he would not rise from the ashes, his body was hacked to pieces and scattered all over the terrain.

Today, near the Taklakot market, there is a small monument which stands testimony to the gory battle which was fought here over a hundred and fifty years back. The monument has been built on some of his remains. Pranavananda's "Kailash-Manasarovar" has it that some of his flesh is still preserved in the Simbiling and the Sakya monasteries and his armour, shield and weapons retained as trophies in some monasteries of the Manasa Khanda. The monument is unique in the respect that it is dedicated by the Tibetans to the bravery of an enemy General. I haven't heard of a monument with a similar dedication in existence anywhere else.

Unfortunately, it also turns out that a typical Kailash-Manasarovar yatri hasn't heard of Zorawar Singh, much less of his exploits. I would strongly recommend a brief stop-over at the Zorawar monument if time and inclination permit. History and geography make excellent teachers provided the student is prepared to listen to their silent, yet profound teachings.

## Telephoning India from Taklakot

International phone calls may be made from a Post Office-cum-Telephone Exchange located very close to the Pulan Guest House. Monday is the weekly holiday. It must be appreciated that the telephone exchange in Taklakot is quite spic, span and a state-of-the-art. The town is practically in the middle of nowhere, still, communication facilities are absolutely first rate. That, they are a little expensive, is a separate question altogether. Phone tariffs are about US $ 7 (about Rs. 250) per minute and in telephoning Mumbai, the caller does not need to holler into the instrument. In fact, the recipient of my call could hear the sound of the air-conditioning in the background. However a 1-2 second delay in completion of speech and arrival of response, similar to calling the USA, is noticed. The Exchange may also be opened on Mondays in case of emergencies. Not many people live in Taklakot, and the locals try to help as much as possible. Insist on paying in Yuan, it is a little cheaper that way (50 Yuan, approx. Rs. 210 per minute).

It might also be worthwhile retaining tokens of Chinese currency and postal stamps for archival value. These may be obtained from the Post Office. When I requested the Postmaster to postmark some stamps for me, he looked at me a little suspiciously first, but later agreed to do it.

## Separation of Groups in Taklakot

After spending a few days in Taklakot, it was time to move on. By now, the Liaison Officer of each group had got to know everybody fairly well and divides the group into two for the sake of trekking and accommodative convenience. One group goes to Kailash first while the other goes to Manasarovar. The Kailash trek is the high altitude trek as compared to the Manasarovar parikrama. Generally, the logic is such that senior people and those who are still in the process of acclimatising to the altitudes, are sent to Manasarovar first while the fitter ones go to Kailash. However, distributions also had to be made equitable.

For every four senior people chosen for Manasarovar, one young man was chosen as an escort. A similar sizing was done for the Kailash group. There were a lot of statistics to handle and our Liaison Officer was continuously shuffling between sheets of paper, marking ticks and crosses against each name.

When it came to announcing the teams, there was some amount of displeasure. Many of those selected for Kailash wanted to go to Manasarovar first and those selected for Manasarovar wanted to visit Kailash first. Many convincing arguments were put forth in favour of each point of view, but our Liaison Officer was firm. I was assigned to the Manasarovar group. I was very happy, I wanted to go to Manasarovar first.

**Planning for the Next Eight Days**

It was decided at the time of separation of the groups that all trekkers would first be taken to Zaidi, a camp on the western shores of the Manasarovar. The Taklakot-Zaidi distance was about 100 km and would be covered by bus. The bus route would be along the Gurla Mandhata range and would traverse the eastern shores of the Rakshas Tal and arrive at Zaidi in about two and a half hours. Yatris would spend some time at Zaidi. The yatris arrived at Zaidi at about 1.00 p.m.

After spending some time at Zaidi, the group moved on to Horche, a small town along the north-eastern edge of the Manasarovar. The bus travelled over the Ganga-Chhu and reached Parkha which is the junction of the three corridors to Kailash-Manasarovar: the Lipulekh-Gurla Mandhata corridor, the Ladakh-Gartok corridor and the Lhasa-Tirthapuri corridor. From Parkha, the bus turned eastwards to the town of Horche (or Hore) located about 20 km from Parkha and 35 km from Zaidi. The group chosen for the Manasarovar parikrama would be left here while the group selected for the Kailash parikrama would be taken to Tarchen again via Parkha, then northwards, for the next 32 km until the market at Tarchen came into sight.

To highlight a few points during the passage from Taklakot to Horche, Taklakot lies at an altitude of 15,500 feet, Zaidi at 15,000 feet, Horche at 14,950 feet and Rakshas Tal at an average altitude of 14,950 feet. The Manasarovar is bigger than the Rakshas Tal, but the Rakshas Tal is longer. The Manasarovar overflows into the Rakshas Tal through the Ganga-Chhu which is a sub-terrainian sluice. In the transport from Parkha to Horche, the trekkers cross the Kung lung which ultimately connects with the Manasarovar to the south and to the Indus on the north. The Manasarovar has no islands in its midst, while the Rakshas Tal has two. The Sutlej arises from the Western shores of the Rakshas Tal while the Manasarovar gives rise to seventeen rivers of which the Tsa Tsangpo (Brahmaputra) and the Karnali are the most prominent. The Manasarovar does not receive water or ice melting at Kailash whilst the Rakshas Tal does. There are several more peculiar and interesting points which will be discussed at their points of greatest significance.

A sketch of the trekking distances in Tibet is presented in Fig. 28. The altitude of each point has been stated both in feet and in metres, as also the distance of each point from the Indian border and from New Delhi. The relative "level of difficulty" in trekking each segment can also be known from this sketch. The axes have been so chosen that as a thumb rule, if the rise or fall of the graph is more than its spread, the trek is difficult to negotiate.

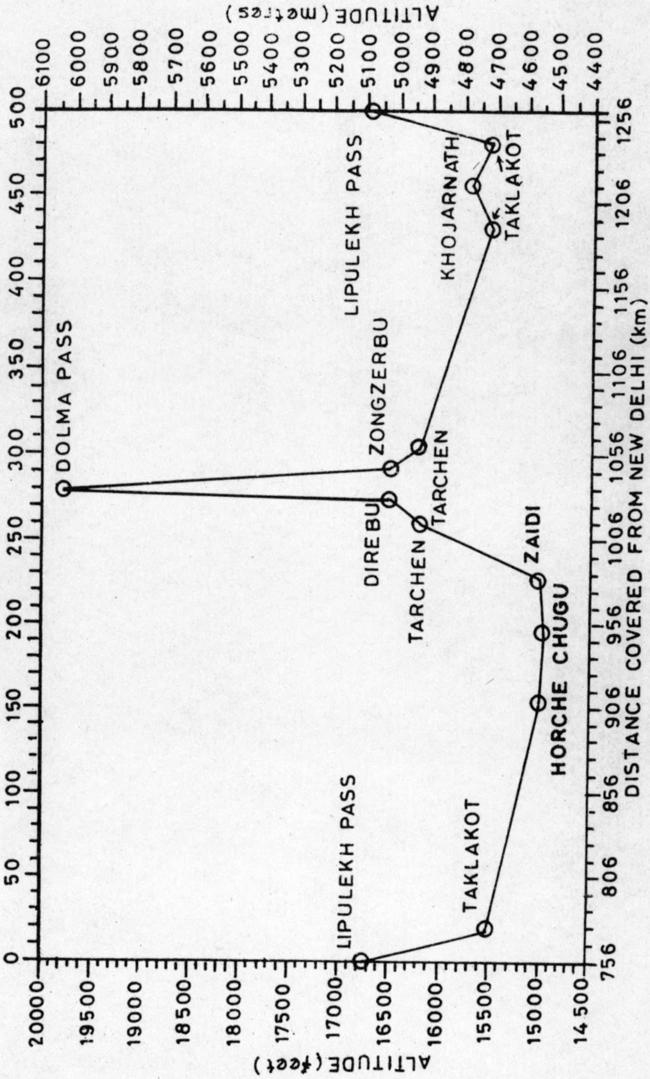


**Fig. 28. A Destination-Distance-Altitude-Inclination map of the Tibetan section of the Kailash-Manasarovar Yatra.**

5

# The Kailash Parikrama

Quite deliberately, I choose to talk about Kailash first, though I performed the Manasarovar before coming to Tarchen. The reasons for this are two-fold. One: the sheer convenience of talking about Kailash first and Manasarovar later so as to maintain the Kailash-Manasarovar sequence. Two: Reserving the best description and photographs for the end so that I am always assured of the reader's attention.

The yatris were brought to Tarchen from Horche or Zaidi and accommodated in the only permanent lodging in the town. The rest house had about 20 rooms, each of which could accommodate four trekkers. Our group of fifteen was assigned four rooms and we were given an extra room for cooking. This was the first time that the trekkers would be cooking their own food. The caretaker had provided us with a few large pots and pans and a kerosene operated stove. The stove resembled a welder's torch in operation, design and flame length and the nozzle turned almost through 90 degrees to focus on the user's beard every time minor adjustments and tuning had to be made. To avoid cuts and nicks and long healing times and additionally, to provide a sun burn cover, we chose not to use our shaving instruments for the duration of the trek. We were almost to regret this decision for in my opinion, there is nothing quite as readily inflammable as a long beard. The sight of men rushing to the water fountain located in the middle of the camp, reminded one of the Thomson twins in Tin-Tin comics, and also evoked a lot of laughter from the Tibetans. Men with beards stayed away from the stove after a few incidents of this sort.

Cooking duties were assigned to all. I was given the responsibility of arranging for hot water for washing and preparing tomato soup for everybody in the group. A few ladies shouldered the responsibility of making *khichdi*. Subrahmanyam made the porridge and Sukumar Das was entrusted with the task of serving the yatris. Regardless of what the reader might have heard from earlier Kailash yatras, we had a very good time with regard to meals and chose to spend many a while in the make-shift kitchen preparing exotic fare. The ladies in our group had finely honed culinary skills and they always had something in reserve for the numerous, perennially hungry, Tibetan children who came knocking at the kitchen door.

The rest house was very large. It also had a garage and a car wash where long distance journey vehicles were attended to. Due to an influx of tourists from Lhasa, many of whom cover the 1300 km distance in several hours of continuous driving, vehicles arrive in badly battered shape. It has suddenly become big business in Tarchen to deal in automobile servicing and overhaul. Most of the vehicles are reconditioned Toyota Land Cruisers or Mitsubishi Pajeros and perhaps these are the only vehicles that could stand the sort of treatment they are subjected to.

By the time we had got ourselves organised it was about 6.00 p.m. The rest house was located almost at the foothills of the Holy Mount Kailash and provided for a delightful Kailash viewing from the South. Though the mountain was at least ten kilometres away from the camp, even by the shortest route, its dome loomed large over the camp and emanated a radiance towards the late evening.

Later in the day, the 'Yak Union' came to meet our group and offered their services and those of their cuddly looking beasts for the Kailash parikrama. Every trekker looked at the yak with a new curiosity for nobody had seen anything of the sort earlier. There was no look of intelligence anywhere on the yak's huge body, but the creature looked as sturdy as a battle tank. Fifteen yaks were hired for the yatris and seven more for the luggage. The hiring charges were to be 50 Yuan (approx. Rs.

215 per day) and the Kailash parikrama was scheduled to last three days. It was decided that the yaks and the yakmen would meet us a kilometre ahead of Tarchen, in the direction of Direbu. Direbu was to be the halting place after the day's trek.

The rest of the day was spent in watching the changing moods and colours of Kailash from the Tarchen camp, as the sun approached its setting. At about 10.00 p.m., the caretaker delivered a huge thermos of hot water to each room to facilitate a basic washing and rinsing the next morning. The next day's trek held a great fascination. We had come from a great distance and had waited very long to have a closer glimpse of Mount Kailash. Now, it was to become a reality. Over the next few days, we would think of nothing else and would fully soak in the juices of the Kailash adventure.

An accurate trekking map of Mount Kailash, based on ascertained measurements and marked positions has not yet evolved. A primitive sketch based on schematic representations and approximations from several authors has been suggested and presented in Map 1. However, potential trekkers are advised that this map is only indicative and not geophysically exact.

**Tarchen to Direbu**

The next day, after a quickly assembled breakfast at 9.00 a.m., the yatris left Tarchen for Direbu. In this segment, we would rise from an altitude of 16,200 feet to an altitude of 16,500 feet over a distance of 14 km through frequent upward and downward inclines. The trekking time would be about 9 hours, inclusive of a 30-minute rest at Choku Gompa near the settlement of Nyanri and a 2-hour cooking and lunch interval on crossing the Dung lung and Bei ling rivulets.

The yatris reached the rendezvous point at about 9.15. Towards 9.30, we saw an army of yaks and yakmen approaching us, kicking up a lot of dust as they drew closer. They had already picked up our luggage from the camp at Tarchen and had come to get us mounted on the yaks. I chose to walk for as long as I could, but had hired a yak for three days in case I were to need one later on. The yakmen were a towering warrior clan, each armed with an authentic Tibetan sword. They surveyed us from head to toe and beckoned us on. Many of them responded to the name of 'Pema' which I assume must be a form of address rather than a name. The yakmen chose their customers and allowed only a likeable sort to mount their beast.

**Some Tips on how to Handle Yaks**

Let's get this straight: When it comes to yaks, there are no recipes to ensure a good yak behaviour. One can only pray and hope to escape with as little injury as possible. A horse is several times more intelligent and trustworthy than the hero of our story. When a yak has to squeeze through narrow pathways between overhanging cliffs, or jump over small streams or climb upon a huge boulder or shake its body free of flies, it takes excellent care of itself. Its feet grip the terrain exceedingly well. Of the 25 yaks that I closely observed for the three days, not once did I see any hesitation in their stride. The beast could hold its entire weight on the strength of its grip. Now, here is where the trouble begins: the yak is supremely confident of its trekking and climbing abilities and looks after itself very well. Unfortunately, when it starts squeezing, leaping, plunging, bolting and contorting, it forgets that it has a passenger on its back. Even if the passenger starts screaming and shouting, the yak gives the impression that the passenger's safety is not of his concern. Very frequently, the passenger is tossed like a ribbon into the winds. Yatris have been hurt, injured, maimed and crippled by the beast's behaviour. The yak also perspires a great deal as a result, the smooth skin and the hair over which the saddle has been bound, get the saddle to slide off the yak's back. Before the yatri realises it, he has been neatly deposited on to the ground.

Climbing up, and staying up a yak is no mean task; it must rank with the fine arts. The beast has no reins and no stirrup and only has a large wooden saddle with a curved grip. The yatris are to hold on to the grip and hold on for dear life. The yak has an amazing ability to climb upto 4 feet with each step with the result that the beast's body can almost be bent into a right angle between the head and the torso. When the yak

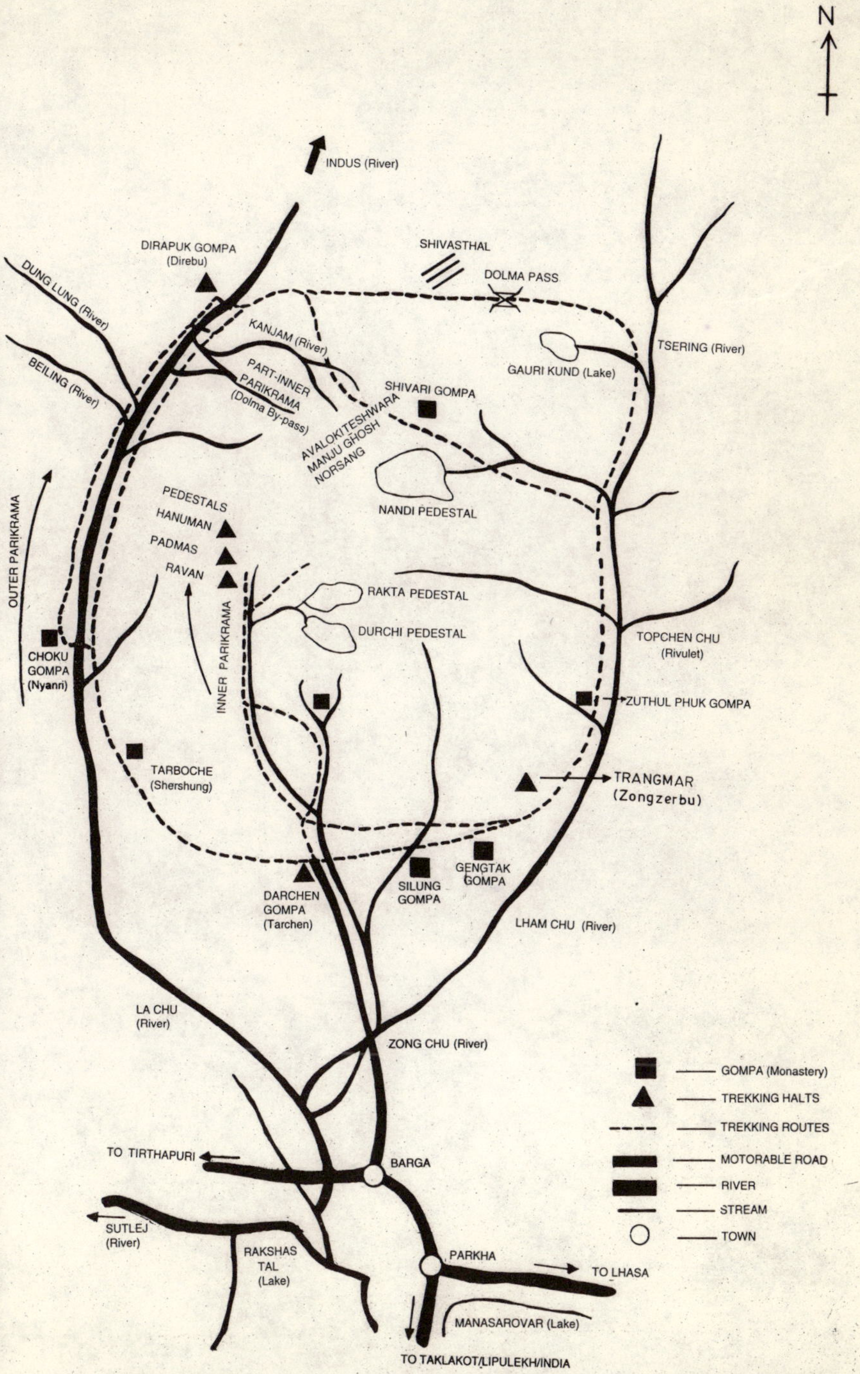


**MAP 1 : A PRIMITIVE TREKKING MAP OF MOUNT KAILASH AND ITS IMMEDIATE NEIGHBOURHOOD.**

makes a movement as sudden as the one described, the saddle, positioned centrally on its back, becomes tangential to its body arch. With no stirrup to protect him from slipping backwards, the typical yatri is found to slide down the yak's back, over his smooth and sweat laden hair and bump onto the ground through a vertical fall of three feet. The yak is a crazy creature, so to say. One moment it likes you, which is when it gives you a long, blank stare; the other moment, it decides that you were meant to be knocked down and without the slightest provocation, charges at you like a runaway locomotive and tosses you into the wind.

Yaks also play power equations with each other. The games are not of a casual one-upmanship, they can get to be very nasty at times. By the time the yatris get on to the yak's back, the yaks among themselves, have chosen their leader and hierarchy for the day. Yaks often walk in a single, or sometimes, in two files, with each yak's head positioned at or near the previous yak's rear legs. A superior yak may walk past, alongside or even across the junior's path with impunity, but if the lower order beast were to do the same, the senior would buffet him in the rib cage with his horns and fell him and his passenger. I have seen however, that hierarchy is changed each day. My yak, whose name was 'Hamta' got me by default. Since I had chosen to walk some distance on the allotment day, the smaller, more innocent yaks were all taken by the yatris and the only beast that remained was this seven feet tall, 600 pound monster who had one broken horn and a squint eye. Hamta was the unquestioned leader for the first two days and bullied and intimidated the other yaks no end. On the third day, Subrahmanyam's yak decided it had taken enough of Hamta's nonsense and decided to fight. Both of us were on our yaks when this happened. Hamta got the shorter end of the stick in the fight and with this defeat, he lost his crown, as well as his popularity with the she-yaks. Hamta licked his wounds, sulked and preferred to come in last. I had got to be a little friendly with the yakmen by this time and they started calling me 'Po-Po' after this incident. I somehow felt like Kit Carson though I still haven't been able to figure out what the name means.

Yaks also horse around with each other. They snort, and playfully hit each other with their horns positioned at each other's rear legs and try to catch the other by surprise. This form of greeting can be very effective in sending the recipient bolting straight ahead at breakneck speed. And they do it all so playfully, but the yatri, by the end of the second day has decided that 'doesn't matter if I drop dead while walking, I am not going to sit on this beast ever again'. I think yatris should be a little more sporting.

So what is the punch line when it comes to yaks? Hire one by all means, you never know when you will need one; but walk as much as you can until you find that you can take it no more. Very few people actually complete the entire parikrama on föot. In the event that you must use the yak's services, make it amply clear to the yakman that he is solely responsible for your safety and that bad yak behaviour will mean that he doesn't get paid. Good behaviour may be rewarded with a 10 per cent bonus. In the entire group, Sukumar Das was one person who never fell off any yak. He chose not to talk to anybody, for this might divert his attention and always ensured that the yakman was at his beck and call. How he managed it, remains a great mystery; but the fact of the matter is his clothes were never dusty or torn and he always arrived at the destination as if in readiness to go to the Opera House.

**Approaching Direbu**

After traversing a few hilly cliffs and descending some steep gradients, the yakmen decided to take a short break near the Choku Gompa. The Gompa is situated at the edge of the La Chu stream which comes from the direction of Direbu as a result of snow melting on the Kailash and ultimately drains to the Rakshas Tal after meeting the Zong Chu near Barga (not Parkha). The Nyanri Gompa is one of the better known gompas in the Kailash Khanda and is located 4 km away from Tarchen. Travelling on a yak, it takes about 2 hours to reach Choku from Tarchen. The yakmen take their beasts to the water for a drink whilst the yatris exchange notes on sightir.gs and musings in the section of the trek just gone by.

The view of Mount Kailash that one gets from Tarchen is of the southern face which gives the impression of the entire peak being a globular dome-like structure. The mental picture that the yatris have is that the globe must be three-dimensional. There is no reason to question this perception even upto and a little beyond the Choku Gompa.

On moving from Choku Gompa half-an-hour later, the terrain becomes a little uneven. Progress is slowed down so that people on yak and people on foot may stay together. Suddenly, a facet of Kailash becomes visible from between two obstructing mountains. This is the western face of Kailash. The mountain is at least 10 km away from the point of photography, but its magnetism and pull make distances irrelevant. The pearly white snow topping on the mountain adds to its majesty and may be regarded as its crowning glory. This facet of Kailash, i.e., the western face keeps peeping out between mountains to gently remind the trekkers of its presence, as they go about the peak in the clockwise parikrama.

Fig. 29 shows a view of the snow-clad Holy Mount Kailash from a point midway between Tarchen and Direbu. This is the western face of the mountain. The sight of this vanilla topped ice-cream cone in the midst of a bald mountain range, is a treat for sore eyes and the trekker, draws strength from this sighting and his otherwise listless (by now it has usually become so) walk acquires a new bounce. The mountain is at least 10 km away from the point of photography and towers over its neighbours by over a kilometre in the vertical.

After trekking for about two hours more, the yakmen decide it is time for lunch. The beasts are unbridled near a patch of greenery at the confluence of the Dung lung and Bei ling rivulets, and left to graze while their masters take their pots and pans out, light a fire and start cooking a meal. The yatris take out their packed lunch and finish eating much before the yakmen have got their meal ready. The yakmen`s meal consists of smoked meat with yak butter. They prepare yak cheese, tie the pieces onto a string and wear the string like a necklace. Every now and then, they pop in a chunk while on the move. Their's is a high protein, high fat diet. In the meantime, the yatris chose to take a stroll in the immediate vicinity of the resting place. Occasional bits of greenery and a rare animal or bird sighting provided an extra bit of excitement in the trek. Direbu was still about 6 km away. By a crude calculation, it would take us about 3 hours more before we ended the day's trekking.

Finally, we started the last lap of the day's trek and traversed along the right bank of the La Chu. Alternatively, Direbu, could also be reached along the left bank. We saw a few monks walking towards Tarchen from Direbu along the opposite bank. On our left, were huge mountains massifs, dark brown in colour. P.T. Shastry who was very quick with his camera brought to our notice, a very unusual sight high up in the brown mountains. On straining our eyes, we could see six deer one behind the other walking away from us. Their colour was such that they blended most readily into the mountains and a topological or colour contrast necessary for a good photograph was not available. Our guide, Mr. Chang told us that these were likely to be musk deer and such sightings were frequent in these parts. I have been wanting to establish the veracity of the guide's claim ever since I came back to Mumbai. Musk deer sightings in Tibet have not been listed in my Zoological Atlas. I wonder if my Atlas is out-of-date. I am quite certain now, that the animals might have been the baral, the mountain sheep which resemble a fox.

After trekking for almost two and a half hours, we came to the Kanjam rivulet which signifies the proximity of the Dirapuk Gompa at Direbu. The fast flowing streams were crossed and we approached the northernmost point in the Kailash parikrama and were presented with the opportunity to catch a glimpse of the northern face of the mountain. An what did we see? We saw that Kailash was not a three-dimensional globular dome, instead, when viewed from the north, it seemed a concave structure and that water flow directions on its northern face could be charted as vertical lines. Several photographs taken from different angles, (figures 30-32) at different hours of the day will illustrate the point.

*Fig. 26.*

Fig. 27

*Fig. 29.*

*Fig. 31.*

*Fig. 33.*

Fig. 34

However, the question of geodesicity apart, the northern face of Kailash acquires brilliant hues, shades and colours depending upon how close the angle of incidence of the sun's rays is to the angle of grazing incidence. Some of the photographs used in this section might highlight this point.

A few structural engineers and scientists in our trekking group casually remarked on the mechanical stability of a simulated structure shaped like the Kailash. If a metallic plate, somewhat convex-o-concave from the south, a little tilted and somewhat directionally biased southwards, with its height and width of a few kilometres, but its thickness insignificant in comparison to its other dimensions, were made to stand on its edge and exposed to strong winds and geological forces along the north to south direction, the mechanical stability of such a structure when strained, would be cause for concern. There is however, a major flaw in the above thesis, which is what we discussed in the rest room at night and that is: the range of mountains surrounding the Kailash, in its almost close contact proximity, shield almost 80 per cent of its height from disrupting forces and ensure that the stresses are never focused at a critical point so as to induce a strain development. As a result, the suggested simulated model is invalid.

Kailash had provided us with food for thought, it was now time to provide food for our stomachs. The usual allocation of duties meant that I was to prepare the soup once again. We had a quick meal and spent some time pensively studying the next day's route. Tomorrow we would reach the highest point of our journey. We would trudge up the Dolma Pass. The incline would be the steepest that we would ever see. Would we be equal to the task? Almost twenty thousand feet above sea level would prove to be a test even for the fittest. We decided to stop worrying: Tomorrow's problems would be addressed by tomorrow's solutions.

**Direbu to Zongzerbu**

The trek from Direbu started very early in the morning at about 7.00 a.m. Chinese time so as to cross the Dolma Pass by

10.00 a.m. The 6 km uphill trek to the Dolma La would take up all of the three hours allocated for it. Today was the day every trekker was waiting for; to benchmark himself as he actually was against the himself he thought himself to be.

The day began very early and by 6.45 a.m. everyone was in a state of physical and mental preparedness. A few, quick early morning photographs of the northern face of Kailash were taken while the yaks and yakmen presented themselves for the day's service. The yatris started moving at 7.00 a.m.

For a good one hour, we were struggling to put as much distance between us and the camp at Direbu, as possible. We couldn't achieve much. The climb was very nearly vertical and the signs of a high altitude fatigue were beginning to tell. The camp always seemed to be vertically below us, and only a stone throw distance away. The dismay lasted until we turned round a corner and continued the ascent along another rock face and couldn't see the Direbu camp any more. We suddenly remembered having read somewhere "Don't look down the mountain when you are climbing up". We bucked up our sagging spirits and looked ahead. The yaks seemed to be in better humour today.

We did not stop anywhere for rest. In any case, a long break was planned at the Pass to facilitate a religious worship and photographic documentation. With this thought at the back of each mind, the yatris extracted every bit of reserve energy and literally dragged themselves over the terrain. The landscape was practically barren all over. A few snow capped mountain slopes and occasional bits of greenery punctuated the desolate landscape. The trekking route was strewn with huge boulders, thousands of them, which had rolled off the mountain tops during a blizzard. The incline was steep indeed. The yaks were steaming at the ears and neck and their breathing had become heavy. Their nostrils had flared and they were unusually subdued. Humans were gasping for breath by now. The trekking process had become very painful and laborious. Nobody dared to stop and lose time and momentum. Howsoever slow, a steady progress was maintained. Nobody thought of shooting pictures, these could be borrowed from somebody else at a convenient occasion. The ascent became steeper. Trekkers would frequently look upwards, and ask their yakmen: "How much further, my good man?" Everytime, the answer would be: "Just a little more". Lungs were pumping to breaking capacity. And then, a red flag was spotted. And then a green spotted. And then several more. "Ah yes, we have arrived" somebody screamed out. And then everybody made a break for it. They all wanted to put the ascent behind them as soon as possible. Everyone reached the Dolma Pass in a scramble. Our watches showed 9.45 a.m. We were well on time.

Fig. 33 is a view of the Dolma Pass, the high point of the entire Kailash-Manasarovar Yatra (19, 800 feet). Direbu to Dolma is a steep ascent and most trekkers believe they will never make it. There is some good news here: Most of the people in our group thought the Lipulekh Pass to be more difficult than the Dolma Pass. The key to a successful Dolma negotiation is to start early from Direbu (by about 7.30 a.m., sunrise occurs at 8.00) while it is still dark so as to cover the 6 km distance by 10.30 a.m. The weather at the Dolma La changes at the drop of a hat and blizzards generally sweep through after 11.00 a.m. Sometimes, it may snow and Dolma may be unapproachable, so ensure that you start descending by 11.00 a.m. In the photograph, the trekking path proceeds from bottom-right to bottom-left through the canopy of colourful ribbons which symbolise a thanksgiving and request for continued divine support. Notice the landslide boulders strewn over the terrain. Kailash lies behind the mountain in the photograph. Also observe the glacier and the gently trickling glacial streams on its either side. The trekking path does not climb the mountain in the picture, it merely skirts around it during the descent.

Once we were secure in the thought of having climbed up the Dolma, yatris started pulling out their cameras and activating their camcorders. The religious ones brought out their prayer accessories and started their worship. Others wandered around the area collecting rock samples and studying the topography. The guides told us we could stay here until 11.00 a.m. The Pass would become inhospitable after this hour once the snows started melting and the winds began blowing. Nobody wanted to claim tenancy rights on the Dolma and we started our downward trek much before this hour. We had to climb down all the distance we had climbed up, so it was expected that even the descent would be tremendously taxing. We soon discovered to our dismay, that all the yakmen had bolted down the descent with their yaks while we were cooling off at the Pass. We were later to learn that this is an implied clause in their service contract, that the services of the yak would not be available during the descent from the Dolma Pass. There was no point in arguing because there was nobody to argue with. Even Chang had made himself untraceable. Two hours later, when we reached the lower altitudes of the river level, we found the yakmen resting on the banks of the Tsering river. They had cooked and eaten their meal and were halfway through their afternoon siesta. The yaks were let loose on the terrain where they were merrily feeding on the grass and chasing each other like a gang of mischievous schoolchildren.

On covering just about a hundred metres down the Dolma Pass, we noticed a large glacial lake, deep down in the valley, towards the right on the trekking route. This is the Gauri Kund and mythology, previous documention and some bits of local folk-lore say that the lake is the bathing chambers of Goddess Parvati and that the set of circumstances which led to Lord Ganesh possessing an elephant head, were enacted here. Parts of the lake are usually always frozen. Evidences of landslides exist in plenty. Some yatris descend to the lake to bathe and collect holy water, others ask their yakmen to do the collecting. An interesting fact is that this lake was sounded for depth measurements as early as in the 1930s by Swami Pranavananda. He carried a small boat with him all the way from India and a prominent businessman from Mumbai was his research sponsor and picked up the tab for all his research expenses. The lake was measured to be 84 feet deep at its deepest point.

Fig. 34 is a view of the Gauri Kund. The holy lake can be

spotted within 100 metres of descent, but is located almost at the bottom of the mountain you have just climbed up. The photograph is taken from a height of about 2,000 feet above the lake level.

We found even getting down to the Gauri Kund to be a much deliberated proposition. We dropped the idea at once when we realised that we would have to climb up the slope once again. Personally, when I compare the effort I take in my field of scientific training with that taken by Swami Pranavananda in his line of work, I feel a trifle guilty of not putting my fullest labours into my occupation. We started along the descent from the Dolma, bypassing the Gauri Kund and moving very cautiously along the steep slopes. It was a long, long walk down, diagonally over a glacier which had begun melting at the edges and over huge boulders, all very cautiously so as to avoid twisting an ankle. Finally, we came to the river front, where we saw the yakmen who looked at us in askance: "Where were you all this time?"

We took a little time to massage our calf muscles and drink a little water from the Tsering, before starting off for Zongzerbu at about 2.00 p.m. The trek to Zongzerbu was along a relatively flat terrain and we made good progress even though we were tired. Zongzerbu was about 8 km ahead from the resting place and on the way, we saw a trekking route coming in from the right to cross our path. This was the Dolma Pass bypass and an excellent short-cut from Direbu to Zongzerbu along a very dangerous trekking path. I will elaborate upon this route in the next few paragraphs. The bypass meets the regular trekking route 6 km before Zongzerbu. As we walked on, we crossed a stream called the Topchen Chu and soon came to Zuthulphuk Gompa which lies East of Kailash. Incidentally, Kailash cannot be seen anymore, it lies hidden from view behind a few obstructing mountains. After about a 45-minute walk from the Zuthulphuk Gompa, we came to the camp at Zongzerbu (or Trangmar) where we were scheduled to halt for the night. Rooms were well laid out with the usual allotment of four people to a room. The Zongzerbu camp is situated on the bank of the Lham Chu and its location is quite picturesque. Zongzerbu lies south-east of Kailash and a sunset over the Rakshas Tal can be beautiful. Incidentally, the Lham Chu from Zongzerbu, the La Chu from Choku Gompa and the Zong Chu from near Tarchen all meet near Barga and flow into the Rakshas Tal.

We made ourselves comfortable in the camp at Zongzerbu and took our time to unwind. The toughest stretch of the journey was behind us. All that remained in the Kailash parikrama, was the descent to Tarchen. Everybody appeared relaxed. We planned for dinner straightaway. We hadn't had any lunch and were quite famished. The day ended before long.

As regards the weather at and before the Dolma Pass, I have known a few people who could not perform the Kailash parikrama and had to return to Tarchen only because of a bad weather at Direbu. I thought such a drastic decision need not have been taken, instead, from Direbu, the route along the Kanjam rivulet, upto the Avalokiteshwara-Norsang rock formations, through the monastery at Shivari and alongside the Nandi pedestal should have been trailed. This route meets the regular Direbu-Dolma-Zongzerbu route about 4 km before the Zuthulphuk Gompa and 6 km before Zongzerbu on the right bank of the Topchen Chu and has a few solid advantages. One, it takes you extremely close to the northern face of Kailash. Secondly, it reduces the overall trekking distance by using the Inner Parikrama route which bypasses Dolma La and Gouri Kund. Thirdly, it is a sacred and a venerated trekking path, not accessible to the religiously and physically underprivileged. The disadvantages are: this route is riskier from the landslides point of view and the trekker ends up bypassing the Dolma La altogether which is a test that every advanced-amateur trekker should subject himself to. However, this route may be preferred to aborting the entire parikrama. It is very important that the guide be well informed and be willing to experiment. Usually, you don't have either and what's more, the language barrier is insurmountable. The punch line is: "Go prepared with your Geography and you will discover interesting bits of History".

**Zongzerbu to Tarchen**

All the trekkers were very relaxed when they were faced with the prospect of trekking from Zongzerbu to Tarchen the next morning. The trek involved a descent from 16,500 feet to 16,200 feet over a distance of 12 km. The journey was a gradual downhill for most of the way, with few or no ascents. A perfectly flat table land could be seen for several miles on the left and the north-western shores of the Rakshas Tal could be seen through a pair of binoculars. The estimated trekking time was about 3 hours and all the trekkers completed this section of the trek without much ado. Kailash could not be seen until we very nearly arrived at Tarchen and as such, this segment of the trek did not hold as much of a romance as some of the earlier sections. For one, the distance was short; secondly, the route was a gentle downhill, third, it was positioned at the fag end of the parikrama and fourth, when a trekker has been through the more difficult, he takes even the less difficult to be very simple. Trekkers were merrily talking and shooting photographs, something they hadn't dared to do while crossing the Dolma.

At Tarchen, we met yatris from the sixth batch, who had just come in from Taklakot and were to begin their Kailash parikrama the next day. We exchanged notes and offered whatever advice we could on trekking through the next few days.

The rest of the day was allocated to spending time the way we pleased. Some yatris went to the local market at Tarchen, the others stayed outside their rooms to catch a glimpse of Kailash changing its colour with the setting sun. And suddenly, there was something quite out of the ordinary. Vishwas Gore, from an earlier batch, thought that the snow on the south-east face of Kailash had accumulated in a very unusual manner so as to look like two faces inscribed in snow. The devout at once called them Shiva and Parvati. I include a copy of the photograph taken by Vishwas Gore and leave it to the reader to interpret it in whichever way he pleases.

There is also a lot of speculation that the mountain forms in the vicinity of Kailash resemble facial features of certain gods (such as Hanuman or Ganesh) or depict their emblems (a trishul or a flagstaff for instance). I must admit that the resemblance is uncanny at a few places, but to me, the entire exercise seems too subjective, for I could not distinguish detail from artifact. I haven't really talked about this aspect anywhere in this book except for one instance where the resemblance was very striking (Fig. 35) and that could be mere coincidence. Sometime in the near future, I would like to go to Kailash once again. This time, not for the sake of trekking but for photography, with even better equipment and along the Inner Parikrama. Maybe then, I might be able to separate the chaff from the grain.

When we reached Tarchen, we had completed one portion of the journey. The next day, we would go to Horche from where the Manasarovar parikrama would begin. Over the last several weeks we had got used to trekking reasonably large distances over mountain terrain. We were to trek 42 km during the first day of the Manasarovar parikrama. The largest distance we had covered in a single day so far, was 18 km between Budhi and Gunji at almost half the altitude. Of course, horses are always available, but a trekker does not go to Tibet to sit on a horse does he?

# 6

# The Manasarovar Parikrama

A great many wonderful theses have been written on the beauty of the Manasarovar. In the four days that I spent at its shores, I must have seen the Holy Lake in many of its colourful forms. The shores were sweltering hot while the waters were freezing cold. Still, the romance of seeing the Lake don new and newer costumes, with changing environmental moods, often with an enticing fickleness, and the very richness of the Manasarovar's celestial wardrobe built up what I may call "the greatest fashion show on earth". In talking about the Manasarovar, my greatest fear is that I may prove unequal to the task, but I will make an attempt nevertheless.

Several years back, in school, my English master tried to teach us about romance literature. He said "Anything which features an adventure is a romance" to which a smart-alec had retorted: "....And every romance is an adventure...." The finer points in the appreciation of spirit were clearly beyond me at that stage, but now after returning from the Manasarovar, I think there may be a small meaning to whatever my master said.

So what is unique about the Manasarovar? Well, it is the only glacial lake in the world which lies at a height of five kilometres above sea level and has water which is sweet to taste. All the lakes in the Ladakh and other regions of comparable altitude have water which is brackish and rich in sulphur.

In case the reader is interested in a few statistics, the Manasarovar is very approximately, circular in shape with a diameter of about 20 km (325 sq. km area, 88 km circumference).

The lake is about 100 metres deep at its centre. Seventeen rivers, including four major waterways, originate radially from the lake. The Kung lung which flows north between the settlements of Parkha and Horche is a source of the Indus. The Tsa Tsangpo flows east and is an origin of the Brahmaputra. The Karnali flows south, into India and joins the Gomti and ultimately the Ganges. The Ganga Chu, a sub-terrainian sluice flows west into the Rakshas Tal from where the Sutlej makes its emergence.

The Lake is said to have been created by Lord Brahma and has more religious stories built upon it than I can ever remember or comprehend. I only remember Manasarovar as one place where I was very happy and content, for no special reason at all! I would like to go again and find out why.

An accurate trekking Map of Lake Manasarovar, based on ascertained measurements and marked positions has not yet evolved. A primitive sketch based on schematic representations and approximations from several authors has been suggested and presented in Map 2. However, potential trekkers are advised that this map is only indicative and not geographically exact.

**Tarchen to Horche**

The yatris who had just completed the Kailash parikrama were brought to Horche in a truck. On the way, we crossed the Kung lung river which originates from the Manasarovar and flows north to meet the Indus. We reached the town of Horche (also Hore, pronounced hoe-ray) which is near the ancient Bonri monastery and lies in the north-east portion of the lake a little distance away from the shores.

Horche is the starting-point in the Manasarovar parikrama. The town only has the bare minimum in facilities. The rest-rooms have only a bed, with space beneath to store your luggage. The rooms are typically 100 sq. feet tenements with 4 or sometimes 5 people to a room. One large thermos flask containing hot water is delivered to each room which must suffice for drinking, morning tea and other morning duties. Water supplements depend upon the goodwill the yatri can generate with the caretaker.

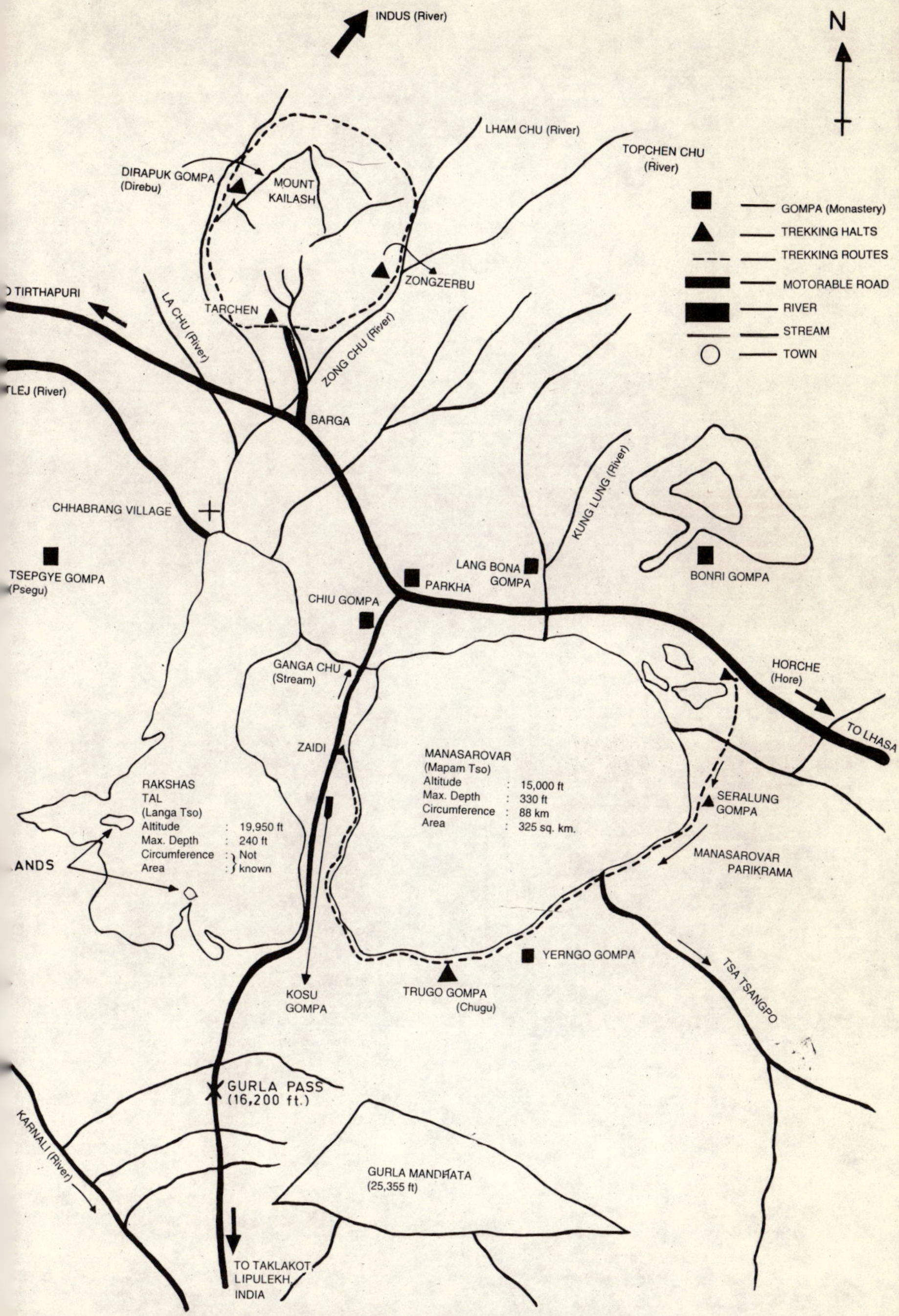


**MAP 2 : A PRIMITIVE TREKKING MAP OF LAKE MANASAROVAR AND ITS IMMEDIATE NEIGHBOURHOOD.**

**Horche to Chugu**

The first day of the Manasarovar parikrama was to be along an extremely flat terrain, along an almost constant altitude of 15,000 feet, for 42 km. The difficulty would lie in walking along the sandy shores of the lake which would be similar to walking on Mumbai's Juhu Beach. The journey would take about 11 hours.

We started from Horche at about 7.00 a.m. Horses were available to whoever wanted to hire them at 50 Yuan per day. One of the first sights that we came across was the towering Fig. 36 shows the Gurla Mandhata and we caught its reflection in the Manasarovar. The image has been captured in a photograph used in this book. Fig. 36 shows the gurla Mandhata range along with its reflection in the hammertone-grey Manasarovar. The Gurla Mandhata massif is over 25,000 feet in altitude and almost equals the height of the Nandadevi. It rises over 10,000 feet above the Manasarovar and is at least 60 km away from the shores of the lake. Its towering height is almost fully reproduced in its reflection which appears to be a faithful facsimile of the original. A cloud line can also be seen in the photograph, which also appears in the reflection. The Manasarovar parikrama starts from the right in the photograph, crosses to the left along the shores and re-emerges on the other side of the lake from the left and crosses all over to the right once again. It is extremely hot along the shores of the lake and temperatures remain at about $45^0$ C for a major portion of the day. The photograph has been taken from Seralung Gompa (between Horche and Chugu) at about 10.00 a.m.

The first halt was at Seralung Gompa, which is a prominent monastery in the Manas Khanda. The Gompa has a very active religious, intellectual and martial arts base even today. Adorning the walls, was a trekking map of Tibet's Ali Province showing all routes. trails and distances in and around the Kailash Khanda, as also those leading into India via the Karakoram, the Lipulekh and through Nepal. I found the map to be most informative. Unfortunately, my camera could not pick up every photographic detail and elevations. It was an exceptionally good relief map.

After leaving the Seralung Gompa, at about 10.00 a.m. we were to walk along the shores of the lake for the next several hours until we crossed the Tsa Tsangpo which originates from the south-eastern edge of the lake. Just before we crossed this river, we stopped for a while to photograph the Manasarovar with Kailash in its backdrop. The photograph included in this section of the book is one of the best in my collection and I would like to remark that Kailash is at least 80 km away from the point of photography and in spite of this large distance, the vertical and horizontal striations along its south-western face are clearly visible.

Fig. 37 is a view of the deep blue waters of the Manasarovar, with the south-eastern face of Kailash in the background. Kailash is the geodesic dome shaped, snow-capped peak occupying the centre of photographic focus within the Kailash range. Observe the colours of the sky as well as those changing within the lake from white to grey to green to emeraldine to blue. Perhaps all the oceans of the world are represented here in colour from the Pacific to the Atlantic to the Indian to the Arctic and even to the Red Sea. The lake is at least 20 km wide and Kailash is at least 60 km from the opposite shore..

We crossed the Tsa Tsangpo where the yatris and horsemen stopped for lunch. It was about 2.30 p.m. now. After an hour's halt we resumed trekking along the lake's sandy shores and crossed the Yerngo Gompa by about 5.00 p.m. Near the Yerngo Gompa, we saw several stones with *Om Mani Padme Hum,* a Tibetan religious salutation, inscribed on them. We continued walking upto Chugu and reached the camp at about 6.00 p.m. The Chugu camp is located at the southern end of the lake and almost at the foothills of the Gurla Mandhata. After having walked the largest distance in the entire trek, we didn't feel up to doing anything else. A meal was hastily put together, some photographs quickly taken while the light was favourable and the day brought to a close.

I must remark that certain places along the Manasarovar parikrama are not very clean. Traces of animal slaughter as an accepted Tibetan ritual exist in plenty. Additionally, a few areas along the lake are found to be teeming with flies which swarm upon the trekkers in their thousands. Fortunately, the flies do not sting, but they do bother the trekker a great deal. The menace is usually confined to three or four places in the parikrama, each, less than half a kilometre long.

Along the Manasarovar, as we also saw during the Kailash parikrama, a few devout Tibetans were performing the prostration circuit. The devotee would cover the periphery of the lake in terms of body lengths and would take a few weeks to cover the Kailash-Manasarovar circuit. I thought, the devotees' determination and ability to stand pain were tremendous.

**Chugu to Zaidi**

The next day, we started our trek at about 8.00 a.m. for Zaidi where our Manasarovar parikrama would end. The Zaidi to Horche segment of the Manasarovar parikrama was completed earlier in a bus. It would not fall on the trekking route because, the Manasarovar is not very approachable along its north-western and northern shores and certain parts are slushy, hence risky to trek along.

The 32 km Chugu to Zaidi distance would take about 7 hours to trek. The beauty of the trek lay in the lake, not in the terrain, which was very much the same all over. It was extremely hot along the shores of the Manasarovar and the parikrama is the occasion when the trekker can get viciously sun burnt if he is not careful. We passed by the Kosu (or Gossul) Gompa located on the western shores of the lake and reached Zaidi at about 3.00 p.m. A little later, we saw a few geese paddling in the cool waters of the lake. Sighting of fauna in the region can be quite a pleasant experience.

Fig. 38 shows a view of the dark blue Lake Manasarovar from Zaidi, the end-point in the Manasarovar parikrama. The Zaidi edge of the lake is a little marshy and ducks and barred geese may be seen paddling in the cool waters. Extensions of the Kailash and the Ladakh ranges are seen along the opposite shores of the lake and the Seralung Gompa is located almost diametrically opposite Zaidi. In this photograph, the viewer looks eastwards. Kailash lies north, Gurla Mandhata is situated to the south, and Rakshas Tal is located west of Manasarovar. The Photograph has been taken at 4.00 p.m. The waters were very cold even at this hour (about $2^0$ C) but a holy dip into the lake was indeed a divine experience.

Over the last few days, I had seen Manasarovar in its many moods and costumes. Later in the evening under a different set of light and cloud conditions, it was to resemble a pool of mercury. The next day when I went into the lake for a religious dip, the waters were freezing cold in spite of the blistering heat outside.

Fig. 39 shows a view of the tranquil, steel-grey Manasarovar at dawn. The lake resembles a large pool of shiny liquid like mercury. It is amazing to know what grazing incidences may do to an otherwise routine landscape. Observe the shimmer at the edge of the lake, it is not a photographic trick, this is how it was in real life. The shores appear brown, the waters silvery and the mountains in the background, blue. It has been fairly well documented that the colours of the Manasarovar waters are the same as those of the clouds above it. Here is another photographic evidence. Large waves are often created during storms. If this picture does not carry an impression of the lake being something out of the ordinary, then the reader is advised not to spend his energies in trekking to Tibet.

Fig. 40 shows a view of some yatris taking a religious dip in the light blue Manasarovar. It is extremely hot (about $45^0$ C) outside the lake and upto anywhere the eye can see, as may be judged from the dazzling sunlight. The time is about 4.00 p.m. and winds are fast, as may be judged from ripples on the lake. The water temperature nevertheless is very close to zero. It takes a great consolidation of mental strength to plunge into the lake and face the winds on the way back. The average teeth-gritting time before plunging was fifteen minutes.

Manasarovar is widely regarded as the seat of sublime sensual pleasure. Every expression tool known to mankind has been employed in its description. Of myself. I find it a little difficult to understand poetic expression, but I can only readily agree to what Dr. Sven Hedin said: "The lake always surprises the expectation but never militates the probability".

**The Enigma of the Rakshas Tal**

The Rakshas Tal is a continuous source of mystery to the Kailash-Manasarovar yatri especially because his contact with the lake over the thirteen days in Tibet does not exceed even thirteen minutes. He knows there is something unusual about the lake, but can't figure out what it could be.

To get to know the facts, the Rakshas Tal is smaller than the Manasarovar, but longer in the north-south direction. Unlike the Manasarovar, it freezes fully in the winters to the extent that one may walk across. The Manasarovar drains into the Rakshas Tal through a sluice at Ganga Chhu, a few miles north of Zaidi. Come to think of it, the Rakshas Tal is the only receptacle for snow melting at the holy Kailash. Even the Manasarovar does not enjoy this privilege. The Sutlej originates here. The Rakshas Tal has two islands in its midst, of which only one is inhabited. Jesuit Antonio de Andrade arrived on the west banks of the Rakshas Tal, over the Mana Pass, in 1626 and built a Church at Chhabrang village, near the Psegu monastery, almost at the source of the Sutlej. The Chepgey Gompa is the only Gompa on the Rakshas Tal and is accorded an exalted status among the monasteries of the Greater Manas Khanda. The greatest depth of this lake is 77 metres. Tempestuous winds blow over the lake at all times and night temperatures in the vicinity of the lake can be as low as -10$^0$ C. Swami Pranavananda says that the changing scenery on the Rakshas Tal is most thrilling and romantically beautiful. And each hour reveals a fresh scene and each bend presents new glimpses of the mountain grandeur and a variety of show that one is bewildered and becomes dumb-struck. Early in the morning, the lake was rough and raging with high roaring waves that the whole surface was white with foam. After a few minutes he was walking inside a gulf where the water was emerald green and even the tiniest pebbles and fish could be clearly seen and photographed. The lake had turned perfectly still. These, and very many interesting facts have been stated in Swami Pranavananda's book, which often makes compelling reading.

However, a typical yatri accords an unholy status to this lake, calling it the *Gateway to Pataal* and taking it to be unholy only because Ravana perchance, did penance in the vicinity. The bigotry has been perpetrated to such an extent, that people do not drink its water for fear of turning into devils or being transported to the netherworld. However, monks, mendicants, scientists and men of a deeper religion who have lived in the area for several years find the Rakshas Tal as enticing and its water as sweet as the Manasarovar. The Oxford School Atlas adopts a middle-of-the-road approach by calling both lakes the Manasarovar Lakes. A view of the Rakshas Tal from near the Kosu Gompa is presented in the accompanying photograph.

Fig. 41 is a view of the Rakshas Tal from near the Kosu monastery. The two islands on this lake may be seen in the photograph. The lake is a little longer (but not bigger) than the Manasarovar. It freezes fully in the winters to the extent that one may walk across. The Sutlej originates from the north-western edge of the lake, located on the opposite shore towards the right in the photograph.

At Zaidi, I had the opportunity to interact with an Earth Scientist from Austria. Over a 12-year period, he has chosen the Rakshas Tal as the theme of his research and documentation and is reported to have spent several days on the lake observing it, studying it and admiring it, just as the Manasarovar has enticed, for the last several centuries. He has chemically tested and analysed the waters of both the lakes and says that compositional differences are too small to allow any conclusions to be drawn. To quote him on the Rakshas Tal "A close scrutiny of the geological maps and the topography suggests that the western shores of the Manasarovar and the eastern shores of the Rakshas Tal might be considered to be closely mating surfaces which would imply that before a geological upheaval separated the two lakes, they were essentially one body of water". This possibility has been very obliquely mentioned in Swami Pranavananda's book.

As regards pure and impure waters, personally, I think it is time that religious bigotry were put in the place it really belongs, that attitudes change and that at least the trekking and mountaineering fraternity stop propagating such malicious information which is scientifically unsubstantiated, howsoever credible it may seem from a religious standpoint.

**On Khojarnath**

Khojarnath is located 26 km away from Taklakot and is the site for one of the few Hindu temples remaining in Tibet. The temple is dedicated to Lord Rama. The idols of Lakshman and Sita may also be seen in this temple. The head priest of this temple is from Nepal however the temple architecture is strikingly Tibetan and like religious protocols in Nepal and elsewhere, leather items are not allowed inside the temple precincts. All along the outer walls of the temple, one may see a series of Tibetan prayer wheels. In the absence of support from religious bodies in India, the temple trustees have been forced to levy a small fee for entry into the temple. Rights to photography may be obtained for 10 Yuan and pieces of silken scarves which were used to adorn the idols before the day's prayer may be obtained for 5 Yuan. Silk scarves with holy Tibetan inscriptions written on them can be had for 10 Yuan. Using the innovative scheme, the trustees have managed to generate sufficient resources to fulfil their religious obligations in a manner well in line with the ideology of the founding fathers.

Fig. 42 shows view of the inner sanctum in the Khojarnath temple. The temple is one of the few remaining in Tibet. Most of the items for religious Vedic worship are seen in the photograph.

Khojarnath was our final port of call in Tibet. Tomorrow, we would prepare to return to India. It was time to snap out of the dream and get back to reality and to Mumbai crowds.

Someday, I would return. And I would try to address everything that I feel I should have done this time. Next time, I would come better prepared.

### A Summary of the Kailash-Manasarovar Yatra

It has been a source of great embarrassment to me that I have thought for several months to effectively summarise my trek to Kailash-Manasarovar. Admittedly, the job was a little difficult. There were too many points to be covered and too few sentences allocated for each. Justice could not have been done.

The text for this book was ready many months ago and I told the publisher I would need time to bring up a good summary. In all my previous attempts, I was never able to write a piece which made me feel happy and I always thought some vital ingredient was perennially missing.

But there has to be a summary. My book wouldn't get published otherwise. So I read the manuscript over and over again and I wrote down the first thought that came to mind.

***You can take a man out of Kailash-Manasarovar, but you can't take Kailash-Manasarovar out of a man.***

## Bibliography

Many of these books are available in the personal archives of Mr. Hiren C. Sampat, Mumbai, an avid collector of all Kailash related documentation, big or small. Complete citation index not available in books of vintage or for limited edition volumes. Comprehensive details are listed where available or possible.


1. Abhayankar Mangala, *Kailash Pradakshina.*
2. Agarwal, V. S., *Matsya Purana: A Study,* 1963, Varanasi.
3. Agarwal, V. S., *Vamana Purana: A Study,* 1964, Varanasi.
4. Agrawal, C. M., *Golu Devata: The God of Justice of Kumaon Himalaya,* 1992, Shree Almora Book Publishers, Almora.
5. Agrawal, D. P., and Kharkwal, J. S., *Kumaun: Archaeology and Tradition,* 1996, Shree Almora Book Publishers, Almora.
6. Ali Salim, Fauna of Manas Khanda, 1946, *Bombay Natural History Society Journal,* Vol. 46, No. 2.
7. Allen Charles, *A Mountain in Tibet,* 1982, London.
8. Arya Trilochan, *Trekking Adventure and Environmental Scenario of Kumaon Himalaya,* 1992. Shree Almora Book Publishers. Almora.
9. Atkinson, E.F.T., *North-West Provinces of India* (14 Volumes).
10. Atkinson, E.F.T., *The Himalayan Districts of the north-western Provinces* (2 Volumes), 1882.
11. Bell Charles, *Tibet: Past and Present,* 1924, Oxford University Press.
12. Bell Charles, *The People of Tibet,* 1928, Oxford-Clarendon Press.
13. Bell Charles, *The Religion of Tibet,* 1931, Oxford University Press.
14. Benjamin, R., *The Art and Architecture of India,* 1953.
15. Scott Berry, *A Stranger in Tibet,* 1992, Harper-Collins Publishers (India), New Delhi.
16. Bhagwan Shri Hamsa, *The Holy Mountain,* 1934, London.
17. Bhatt, S. D., and Pathak, J. K., *Himalaya Environment: Water Quality of the Drainage Basins,* 1992, Shree Almora Book Publishers, Almora.
18. Bole, P. V., and Mehta, *A Himalayan Flowers,* 1985, Tata Press, Bombay.

19. Bower Hamilton, *A Journey across Tibet,* 1893.

20. Bower Hamilton, *Diary of a Journey across Tibet,* 1894, London.

21. Brunton Paul, *A Hermit in the Himalayas,* 1975, London.

22. Burrad, S. G., and Haydon, H. H., *A Sketch of the Geography and Geology of Himalayan Mountains and Tibet,* 1934.

23. Campbell Joseph, *The Masks of God* (4 Volumes).

24. Chamaria Pradeep, *Picturesque Passage,* 1996, Abhinav Publications, New Delhi.

25. Crook William, *Religion and Folklore of North India,* 1926.

26. Dabral, S. P., *Uttarakhand ka Itihaas* (6 Volumes), (in Hindi).

27. Darian, S. G., *The Ganges in Myth and History,* 1978.

28. Das, Sarat Chandra, *A Journey to Lhasa and Central Tibet,* 1902.

29. Date Shankar Sakharam, *Himalaya Darshan,* Part-2.

30. Desideri Oppolito, *An Account of Tibet: The travels of Oppolito Desideri of Pistoia,* 1932, S. J., London.

31. Dilwali, Ashok, *Kumaon Himalaya,* 1993, Shree Almora Book Publishers, Almora.

32. Downson, J., *Classical Dictionary of Hindu Mythology and Religion,* 1913.

33. Edwin Schary, *In Search of the Mahatmas of Tibet,* 1937, London.

34. Eliade, Mircea, *Images and Symbols,* 1952.

35. Eliade, Mircea, *Patterns in Comparative Religion,* 1958.

36. Ekvalls, Robert, *Religious Observations in Tibet,* 1964, Chicago.

37. Feynman Richard P., *Surely You're Joking, Mr. Feynman,* 1985, Bantam Books, New York.

38. Filippi, F., *An Account of Tibet.*

39. Fonia, K. S., *Uttarakhand,* 1978.

40. Garma Chang C. C., *The Hundred Thousand Songs of Milarepa,* 1962, New York.

41. Ghosh, Shambhu Nath, *Kailash and Manasarovar– A Pilgrimage,* 1990, Bardhan Press, Calcutta.

42. Giuseppe Tucci, *Tibet— Land of Snows,* 1967.

43. Giuseppe Tucci, *The Theory and Practice of Mandala,* 1969.

44. Giuseppe Tucci, *Trans-Himalayas,* 1973.

45. Gopinathrao, T. A., *Elements of Hindu Iconography,* 1914.

46. Gorer, Geoffrey, *The Lepchas of Sikkim,* 1990, Gyan Publishing House, New Delhi.

47. Gotami, Govinda Li, *Tibet in Pictures,* 1979, Emeryville Publishers, USA.

48. Goyal, Somesh, *"Journey to Kailash-Mansarovar : Pilgrims Handbook,* 1997, Arya Publishing House, New Delhi.

49. Govinda Angarika Lama, *The way of the white clouds,* 1966, London.

50. Havell, E. B., *The Himalayas in Indian Art,* 1899.

51. Hedin Sven, *Through Asia,* 1899.
52. Hedin Sven, *Central Asia and Tibet,* 1903.
53. Hedin Sven, *Adventures in Tibet,* 1904.
54. Hedin Sven, *Trans-Himalaya: Discoveries and Adventures*— Vols. I-III, 1909, Gyan Publishing House, New Delhi.
55. Hedin Sven, *Southern Tibet* (9 Volumes), 1922, Stockholm.
56. Hedin Sven, *A Conquest of Tibet,* 1935.
57. Heim Arnold and Gansser A., *The Throne of the Gods.*
58. Heim Arnold and Gansser A., *Central Himalaya,* 1936, Reports of the Geological Observations of the Swiss Expedition.
59. Heinrich Harrer, *Seven Years in Tibet,* 1953, London.
60. Herbert Tichy, *The Holiest Mountain,* 1936.
61. Herbert Tichy, *Tibetan Adventure,* 1938, London.
62. Hermans Martin, *The Indo-Tibetans.*
63. Heroor Uma Ashok, *Jai Manas Manastaphara.*
64. Huc M., *Travels in Tertiary Tibet and China,* 1900, Chicago.
65. Hutchinson, J., and Vogel, J. P. H., *History of Punjab Hill States.*
66. Iozawa Tomoya yama-kei, *Trekking in the Himalayas.*
67. Jigmei N. N., Chodra K., Phuntso C. T., Zhen Na, Xiansheng Cai, Chinlei J., and Luosantselei D., *Tibet,* 1981, Bracken Books, London.
68. Joshi, Maheshwar P., *Morphogenesis of Kunindas: A Numismatic Overview,* 1990, Shree Almora Book Publishers, Almora.
69. Joshi, Maheshwar P., *Uttaranchal (Kumaon- Garhwal) Himalaya: An Essay in Historical Anthropology,* 1990, Shree Almora Book Publishers, Almora.
70. Joshi, Maheshwar P., Fanger Allen C., and Brown Charles W., *Himalaya: Past and Present,* 1994, Shree Almora Book Publishers, Almora.
71. Joshi, Maheshwar P., and Joshi, L. P., *Rishi: Uttaranchal Himalaya Society, Culture, History, Archaeology, Anthropology, Art, Botany,* 1995, Shree Almora Book Publishers, Almora.
72. Kawaguchi, E., *Three Years in Tibet,* 1909, Madras.
73. Keay, John, *Where Men and Mountains Meet,* 1977, London.
74. Keith, A. B., *Taitriya Samhita,* 1914.
75. Khembo Sonam Gelzin, *Khochar Purana,* 1758, Ngor Gompa manuscript, Tibet.
76. Khulbe, R. D., *Microbial Activity in the Himalaya,* 1992, Shree Almora Book Publishers, Almora.
77. Konchog Sakai Gelong, and Lodroe Tenzing Choekyi, *The crystal clear mirror of a brief history of Kailash and Manasarovar,* (translated from Japanese by Tshewang Tandiling).
78. Kramrisch, S., *The Hindu Temple,* 1946, Calcutta.

79. Kramrisch, S., *The Presence of Shiva*, 1981. Princeton University Press, Princeton.

80. Landor, A. H. S., *In the Forbidden Land* (2 Volumes), 1898, London.

81. Law, B. C., *Mountains and Rivers of India*, 1968.

82. Longstaff, Tom, *This is my Voyage*, 1950, London.

83. Macgrego, John A., *Tibet—A Chronicle Exploration*, 1970, London.

84. Macdonell, A. A., *A History of Sanskrit Literature*.

85. Manson, K., *The Abode of Snow*, 1955.

86. Marco Pallis, *The Way and the Mountain*, 1960, London.

87. Mishan Ye-Ses-Rgyal and Bstah D. Karru Grubdban, *Sacred Kailash and Manasarovar*, 1979, Tibet House, New Delhi.

88. Misra, N. N., *Source Materials of Kumaoni History*, 1994, Shree Almora Book Publishers, Almora.

89. Moorcroft, W., *A Journey to Lake Manasarovara in Un-Des—A Province of Little Tibet*.

90. Morran, Kerry and Johnson Russell, *Kailash—The Sacred Mountain*.

91. Norbu, Thupten Jigme and Turnbull Colin, *Tibet*, 1969, London.

92. Norbu Dewang N., *History of the Sacred Mountain Tise and Blue Lake Mapham*, 1973, Ed. B. Olschak in 'Mystic Art of Ancient Tibet', London.

93. Oakley, E. S., *The Holy Himalayas*.

94. O'Connor Bill, *Adventure Treks: Nepal*, 1990.

95. *Oxford School Atlas, The*, Oxford University Press, 1993, New Delhi.

96. Pande, D. C., *Dimensions of Agriculture in the Himalayas*, 1995, Shree Almora Book Publishers, Almora.

97. Pande, R. K., *Quantitative Geomorphology of Himalayan Drainage Basin*, 1990. Shree Almora Book Publishers, Almora.

98. Pandey, Badri Datt, *History of Kumaun* (2 Volumes), 1993, Shree Almora Book Publishers, Almora, translated from *Kumaun ka Itihaas*, (in Hindi) 1937, C. M. Agrawal.

99. Pandey, P. C., and Pandey, M. C., *Illustrated Fern Flora of Central Himalaya* (2 Volumes), 1996, Shree Almora Book Publishers, Almora.

100. Poddar, Hanumanprasad, *Sankshipt Shivapuran*, (In Hindi) 1996, Geeta Press, Gorakhpur

101. Poddar Hanumanprasad, *Shivank*, (In Hindi), 1996, Geeta Press, Gorakhpur.

102. Poddar Hanumanprasad, *Kalyan Teerthank*, (In Hindi), 1997, Geeta Press, Gorakhpur.

103. Prajapati, J. M., *Kailash-Manasarovar Alaukīk Yatra*, 1997, Gandhi Impex Publishers, Bombay (in Gujarati).

104. Radhakrishnan, S., *Indian Philosophy* (2 Volumes), 1923, London.

105. Raha, Manis Kumar, *The Himalayan Heritage*, 1990, Gyan Publishing House, New Delhi.

106. Rawling, C. G., *The Great Plateau,* 1905, London.

107. Sah, N. K., Bhatt, S. D., and Pande, R. K., *Himalaya: Environment, Resources and Development,* 1990, Shree Almora Book Publishers, Almora.

108. Sandberg, Graham, *Exploration in Tibet,* 1904, Calcutta.

109. Shipton, Eric, *That Untravelled World,* 1969.

110. Singh, O. P., and Pande, R. K., *Human Habitat in the Mountains,* 1996, Shree Almora Book Publishers, Almora.

111. Smythe, Frank, *The Valley of Flowers,* 1931, A. C. Black and Publishers, London.

112. Snelling, John, *The Sacred Mountain— The Complete Guide to Tibet's Mount Kailash,* 1990, East-West Publications, London (foreword by the Dalai Lama).

113. Stein, R. A., *Tibetan Civilisation,* 1972, London.

114. Subbá, Tanka B., and Datta, Karabuki, *Religion and Society in the Himalayas,* 1990, Gyan Publishing House, New Delhi.

115. Swami Pranavananda, *Pilgrims Companion to the Holy Kailash-Manasarovar,* 1938, Hindi Sahitya Sammelan, Allahabad.

116. Swami Pranavananda, *Exploration in Tibet,* 1942, Calcutta University Press.

117. Tewari, P. C., *Natural Resources and Sustainable Development in Himalaya,* 1995, Shree Almora Book Publishers, Almora.

118. Tolia, R. S., *British Kumaon-Garhwal* (2 Volumes), 1995, Shree Almora Book Publishers, Almora.

119. Varma, Sadhana and Varma Rommel, *Kailash Manasarovar: Ascent to the Divine,* 1985, Switzerland.

120. Vijay Tarun, *Kailash-Manasarovar Yatra: Saakshaat Shiv se Samvaad,* (in Hindi), 1989.

121. Wadia, D. N., *The Himalaya Mountains.*

122. Webber, Thomas W., *In the Forests of Upper India,* 1902, London.

123. Wessels, S. J. C., *Early Jesuit Travellers in Central Asia,* 1924.

124. Wilson, Christopher Grey, and Blamey, Marjorie, *The Illustrated Flora of Britain and N. Europe,* Collins-Howard Clase, London (illustrated documentation on about 2500 plants).

125. Woodroffe, John, *The Principles of Tantra* (2 Volumes), 1914.

126. Zachner, R. C., *Hinduism,* 1966, Oxford University Press, Oxford.

127. Zimmer Heinrich, *Myths and Symbols in Indian Art and Civilization,* (In Hindi) 1945, New York.

# Index


Administrative Protocol. 37
Afghanistan, 83
Aksai Chin, 36
Allahabad. 79
Almora, 28, 32, 36, 38-40
Annapurna, 48
Auli Slope, 74
Avalanche, 55
Avalokiteshwara-Norsang, 102

Basti Ram. 83
Bei ling. 91. 95
Beijing. 79
Bhowali, 39
Bindakoti. 51
Bonri Monastry. 106
Border.
  India-Nepal. 23
  Police. 72-73
Botanists. 57
Budhi. 25-26. 54-57. 59-60. 104

Cameras &
  Camcorders. 72. 80. 96
Chandigarh. 79
Chandrabindu. 70
Chaukori. 40
Chhia Lekh Pass. 58-60
China. 79
Chinese,
  Army. 81.83
  Bank. 80
  Currency. 84
  Customs. 82
  Food. 80
  Food Stal. 79
  Visa. 38
Choku Gompa. 94. 95. 102
Chugu Camp, 108
Colorado-Grand Canyon. 23

Dharchula, 28, 38, 40-43, 62, 68
  Indian, 42
  Nepal, 42
Dirapuk Gompa, 96
Direbu, 25, 27,91, 94-98, 101-102
Distance,
  Lipulekh-Taklakot, 25
  Taklakot-Horche, 25
  Tarchen-Taklakot
  ...Lipulekh, 25
  Zaidi-Tarchen, 25
Dolma La, 96, 99
Dolma Pass, 21, 25, 28, 64, 67.
  99, 100-103
Dung Lung, 91.95

Elois, 77
Explorer,
  Mongol. 32, 35
  Russian. 32, 35
External Affairs, Min. of...
  21. 35. 37. 41, 44

Flora & Fauna, 23
  Flora, 55, 57
Floral Beauties, 56
Flowers. 57-58
  Chrysalis Imperialis
    Variety, 57
  Himalyan Betony, 57, 58
  Himalyan knotweed, 57
  Himalyan Hogweed. 57
Foreign Exchange. 37-38

Gajraula. 39
Gala, 25, 26, 49-50. 53, 64
Ganga (Ganges). 39, 106
Ganga Chhu, 85-86, 106
Garibians, 58, 60
Gartok, 31, 35, 83

Gauri Kund, 100, 107
Geographic Mercators, 36
Geologists, 19
Golf Course, 47
Gomti, 106
Great Panjab, 83
Great Tibetan Plateau, 73, 79
Greater Manas Khanda, 111
Gunji, 25, 26, 62, 64-66, 72, 104
Gurla-Mandhata, 21, 75, 107, 108, 110
Gurla Mandhata Range, 84

Haryana, 83
Hedin, Sven, 17, 20, 35, 36, 111
High Blood Pressure, 38
High Glucose in Blood, 38
Himachal Pradesh, 83
Himalyan Flowers, 23
Himalyan Non-Basaltic Mountain, 46
Himalayas, 15, 39
Historians, 19
Horche, 31, 35, 85-86, 89, 106-107, 109

Immigration Formalities, 80
Indemnity Bonds, 37
Indianapolis-500, 23
ITBP Hospital, 37, 61
  Camp, 62
ITBP (Jawans) 41, 65-68, 70-73
  74-75
Indian Traders, 31
Indo-Tibet Trade
  Licenses, 41
Indus, 32.106
International Border, 65
Iron Fist in a Velvet Glove, 73

Jabalpur, 23
Jammu & Ladakh, 82
Jipti, 51
Junglechetti, 49

KMVN, 37, 39, 40, 41, 43, 46
  48, 55, 60-61, 66, 69
Kailash (Tarchen), 16, 23-24, 33-35,
  43-45, 53, 55, 66, 75, 82, 84-86, 89-91,
  94-99, 101-104, 108
  More Routes, 31
  Mountain, 23
Kailash Khanda, 76, 94, 107
  (Tarchen)
Kailash-Manasarer,42, 46, 68
Kailash Manasarovar Attitude, 48
Kailash-Manasarovar
  Rakshas Tal Triangle, 31
Kailash-Manasarovar Trek, 19, 56,58
Kailash Manasarovar Yatra, 16, 17
  18, 20, 21-25, 26, 31, 35, 36,
  39, 41, 64, 70, 99, 111, 114
  Categories, 20
    Adventure Book Segment, 20
    Pravananda Class, 20
    Sacrosanct, 20
  Mandal, 18
  Wildlife Sororities, 20
  Risk & Challenges, 20
  Trek, 19
Kailash Parikrama, 21, 44, 76, 84-85
  89-91, 96, 102-104,
  106, 112
Kailash Range, 21
Kalapani, 66-69
Kaliganga (River) or Kali, 23, 42, 47, 51-
52, 59, 60-61, 66-69
Kang-Rinpoche, 31
Kanjam, 102
Karakoram, 107
Karnali, 86, 107
Kashmir, 57-58, 83
Kathmandu International Cafe, 42
Kazakh, 77
  Nomads
Kazakhstan, 32, 35
Khojarnath, 25, 113
Kjelstrom, CJ (Lt.), 36
Kosu Gompa, 109, 112
Kumaon Hills, 39
Kung Lung, 106
Kuti-Kaliganga Confluence, 61
Kuti River, 61
Kyrgyzstan, 32, 35

La Chu, 94, 96, 107
Ladakh, 83
Lakhanpur, 51, 52
Lamari, 54, 55
Land Rovers, 35
Land Slides, 66
Lee Falk's Portrayal, 53
Lipulekh Glacier, 74
Lipulekh Pass, 16, 25, 32, 62, 64, 65, 68,
  71-75, 99, 107, 79
    Stretch, 62
Lham Chu, 101-102

Lhasa, 32, 90
Lord Brahma, 106
Lord Shiva, 68
Lord Vishnu, 48

M.T.V., 49
Malpa, 25-26, 50, 52-54, 64
Manas Khanda, 83, 107
Manasarovar, 16, 19-20, 31, 35, 80, 83, 84-66, 89, 105-110
  Lake, 23
  Parikrama. 36, 45, 105-109
Mapan Tso, 31
Marco Polo, 41
Mean Sea Level. (MSL), 28
Mitsubishi Pajero, 80, 90
Morloks, 77
Mount Adi Kailash, 61
Mumbai, 23-25, 79, 84, 76, 100, 107
  Lohar Chawl, 42

Najung Jharana, 53
Najunggarh, 52, 53
Nanda Devi, 107
Nandi, 102
Napalchials, 60
Napalchu, 60-61
Narayana Ashram, 45-48
Narkanda Slope, 74
Narmada, 23
Navidang, 25, 26, 39, 65, 68-72, 75
Navidang-Lipulekh, 21
Nepal, 47, 48, 52, 66, 68, 107, 113
New Delhi/Delhi, 25, 28, 38, 39, 62
Norbu, Dewang, 24
Nyanri, 91
  Gompa, 94

Om, 70
Om Parbat, 70-71
Ornithologist, 20

Pajeros, 35
Pakistan, 83
Pangu, 46, 48
Pangla, 51
Pangu, 25-26, 28, 45
Parkha, 31-32, 35, 83, 85, 106
Perth, 79
Phantom Skull Cave, 53
Photographs,-phy,-phers, 52, 55, 57, 59, 61, 66-73, 75, 80, 89, 95-98, 103, 104, 107, 108, 110, 112
Porter's HQ., 42
Pranavananda (Swami), 17, 20, 28, 31, 75, 77, 82-83, 100-101, 112-113
Psegu Monastry, 111
Psoralin, 58
Pulan Guest House, 76, 80, 84

Rakshas Tal, 32, 35, 85-86, 94, 102, 103, 110-112
Rampur, 39
Ravana, 112
River Gone Crazy, 60
River Level, 28
Routes to Kailash Manasarovar, 31-34, 35
  Almora Tarchen, 36
  Dharchula-Lipulekh, 31
  Direbu-Dolma-Zongzerbu, 102
  Indo-Tibetan Trade, 31
  From Kedarnath, 31
  From Ladakh, 31
  From Srinagar, 31
  From Upper Assam, 31
  From Western U.P., 31
  Kalapani-Navidang, 69
  Simla-Srinagar Ladakh, 32
  Ski Route, 75
Rungling Top, 49-50,

Salim Ali, 57
Samuri, 49
Sedimentary Rock
  Deposits, 46
Seralung Gompa, 36, 107-108, 110
Shivank, 20
Shivari Monastry, 102
Simbiling/Sakya monastries, 83
Singh, Zorawar, 82-83
Sirdang, 48
Sirkha, 46-49, 64
Skin Therapy, 58
Sosa, 47
Step by Step-
  Destination, Distance, Tahle, 26-27
Sutlej, 86, 106, 111-112

Tadroopananda (Swami), 47-48
Takla Makan/Gobi Deserts, 32
Taklakot, 25, 27-28, 31, 38, 41, 76, 79, 80-86, 103, 113
Taklakot-Zaidi Distance, 84
Tarchen, 89-91, 94-96, 103, 106

Camp, 91
Tawaghat, 23, 25, 28, 36, 43, 45, 46, 51, 54, 64
Tawaghat-Pangu Stretch, 21, 64
Temples,
  Golu, 40
  Kainchi, 40
  Shiva-Parvati, 67
  Vaishnava Devi, 67
Thanedar ki Chadhai, 25-26, 46 (Pangu)
Tibet, 16, 19, 21, 31, 38, 41, 68, 72-76, 79-80, 82-83, 86, 96, 107, 113
  Ali Province, 20
Tibetan, 83, 89, 90
  Authorities, 65
  Daggers, 82
  Music, 82
  Plateau, 35
  Races, 77
  Rituals, 108
  Sword, 91
  Women, 80
Tilberry Port, 23
  Thames, 23
Time Machine (H.G. Wells). 77
Time Zones, 79
Tirthapure, 83
Tom Sawyer. 15, 67
Topchen Chu, 101-102
Tourist Department.
  J & K, 35
Toyo. 83
Trade Routes. 31
Trek to Kailash-Manasarovar. 19, 29
  For Adventure. 20
  For Documentation. 20
  For Pilgrimage. 20
  For Research. 20
  Difference of Trek, 20
  Other Treks, 21
  Route-Wise—
  Delhi-Almora-Dharchula-Gunji-Lipulekh-Taklakot-Manasarovar-Kailash. 21
    Horche-Chugu Distance. 21
    Gala Malpa Section, 21
    Return Journey Distance. 21
Trekkers, 16, 20, 31, 32, 34-36, 41, 43, 47. 50-53, 57-62, 64, 65, 66, 67-69, 71-75, 86, 89, 95-99, 106, 108.
  Amateur, 16
  Map, 91
  Shoes, 81
  Trekking path, 47, 48, 66, 74
  Trekking Route, 49, 53
Trekking, 41
  Achievements, 19
  Distances, 63-64, 86
  Information, 21
  Information Maps, Absence, 36
  Maps, 36, 91
  Segments, 25
  Routes, 21, 23, 25, 31, 36, 46, 100, 101, 103, 104, 109
Trekking Corridors
  Ladakh Gartok Corridor, 31, 35, 36, 62, 85
  Lipulekh-Gurla-Mandhata Corridor, 31, 35,
  Lhasa-Tirthapure Corridor, 31, 35, 85
Tsa Tsangpo (Brahmputra), 86, 106, 108

Uttarakhand Tourist Dept, 39

Vashikar, R.D., 18
Vyas Cave, 66-67
Vyas Mountain. 66

Walking Skills. 45

Yak union. 90
Yaks. 38. 76. 90-94. 100. 103
Yarkand-Gartok
  Trekking Lake. 35
Yatris. 42-44. 47-48. 61. 66. 68. 72-73. 84. 89, 91, 93, 95, 98, 112
  Haversack, 44
Yerngo Gompa, 108

Zaidi. 44. 85. 86. 89. 109. 110. 112
Zero Area. 41. 42
Zollingkong. 61
Zong Chu, 94
Zongzerbu. 25. 27. 97. 101-103
Zuthulphuk
  Gompa, 101-102

*Fig. 35.*

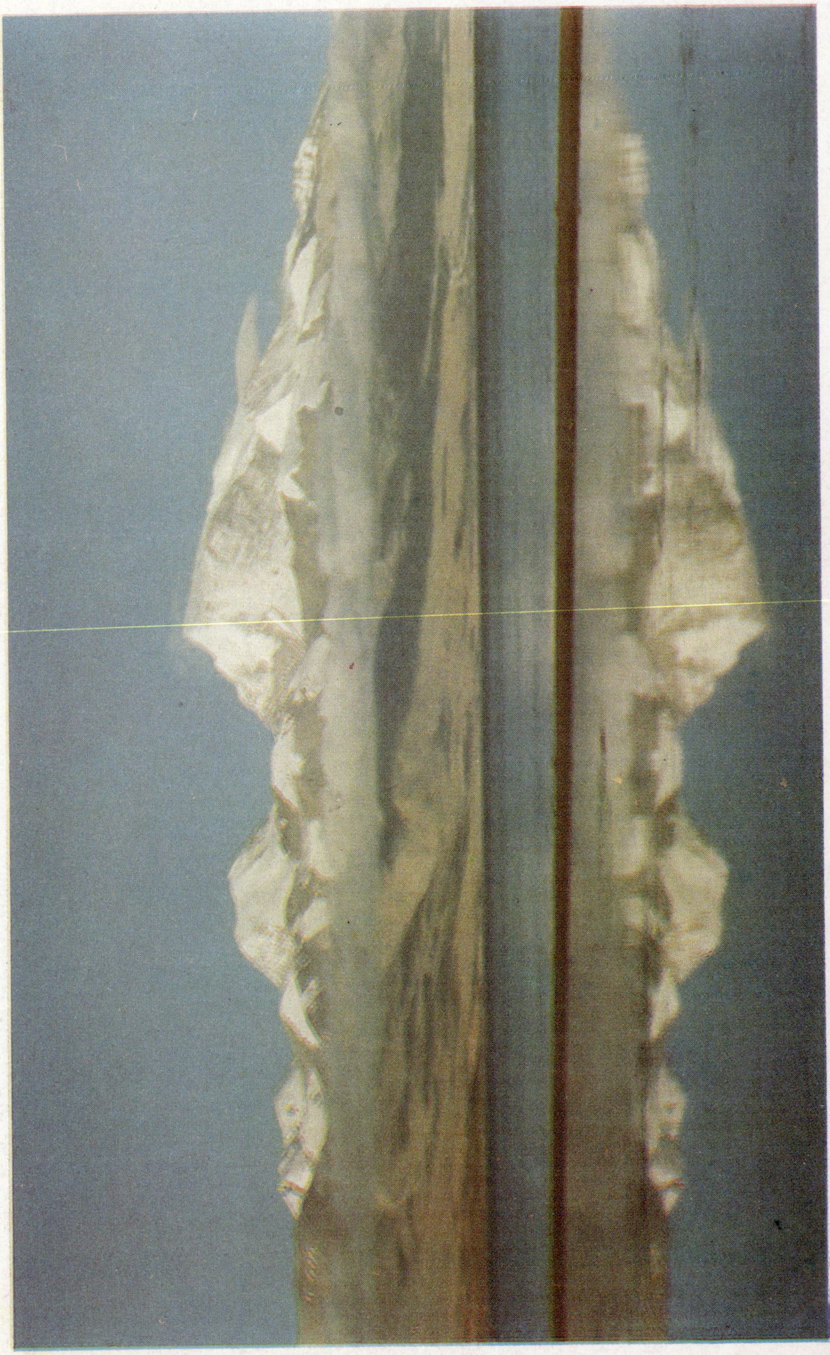

*Fig. 37.*

*Fig. 38.*

*Fig. 39.*

*Fig. 41.*

*Fig. 42.*